Doing God's Business God's Way:

A Biblical Theology of Ministry

by

George J. Zemek

To

Judy, the excellent wife God has mercifully given me. Your love is a priceless gift from Him, and your encouragement and wisdom are mainstays for my ministry. May our Lord continue to bless and use you in His kingdom for His great glory.

Table of Contents

Part II
SALVATION AND SUFFICIENCIES

Part III
SHARING AND SERVING

Preface

The doctrines of grace have fallen on hard times. Even in circles where the sinfulness of sin and the sufficiencies of God, both for salvation and for sanctification, are professed theologically, methodological compromises are nullifying such seemingly hollow creedal affirmations.

It is not so surprising to find those who hold to a high view of man's innate spiritual 'abilities' pursuing after any and every method to try to obtain eternal 'results.' However, it is shocking to see what means are being employed today by increasing numbers of people who profess to hold to man's total depravity and God's sovereignty in salvation and sanctification.

In view of these disturbing phenomena, I would urge every reader to examine himself as a good Berean would, by the standard of Holy Scripture. Are you really *doing God's business God's way* or merely attempting to do His work man's way?

Just a note about the nature of this book. I have striven to avoid technical discussions and the heavy-duty documentations which characterize academic presentations. However, my conclusions on the passages employed represent a detailed spade-work in the Hebrew and Greek texts from which they come. I have attempted to make the discussion throughout as user-friendly as possible in order that 'lay' person and 'professional' alike may consider, and hopefully profit from, its contents. In other words, I have tried to preach on paper.

Nevertheless, in the quotes from Scripture I have often added parenthetical and bracketed comments. In general, the parentheses contain optional connotations for a word, phrase, etc., while the bracketed materials contain various kinds of abbreviated commentary. Sometimes, I translate a verse very literally to try to demonstrate its impact. At other times, I use interpretive paraphrases for the same reason. Occasionally, I do both in the same verse or unit of verses – hopefully there *is* method in my madness! On those occasions when I use a popular modern version of a text, I credit it by a parenthetical notation.

If anyone should be interested in some of the more technical materials which undergirded this book (e.g. dissertation, articles, course syllabuses, etc.)* please write to the address below (this address also pertains to the ordering of copies for other people who might benefit from this book):

Doing God's Business God's Way
P. O. Box 428
Mango, Florida 33550-0428

*Requests for such materials will be granted only when an explanation of the legitimate use of them has been documented.

Introduction

The road I would like to lead us down is both theological and methodological. Although the Bible does not contain a 'how-to' book for the carrying on of Christian ministry, all kinds of methodological implications surface from a biblical (i.e. an exegetical) investigation of the doctrines of God's sovereign grace. The Word of God, from Genesis to Revelation, contains mountain ranges of data on this most vital topic; therefore, I will endeavor to pick out the most conspicuous 'peaks' in each area for examination.

As a point of caution, we must be patient in our methodological quest. The journey will involve several different, though interrelated, expeditions. All of these theological expeditions will begin quite generally; however, the methodological significance of each one of them should become progressively clearer as that particular 'leg' of our journey terminates by merging into the next stage of the overall quest. And, as these stages reach their ultimate destination, the final one will become more transparently methodological.

Or, to use an architectural image to illustrate how I would like to lead us through the Scriptures theologically and methodologically, it may be helpful to envision ourselves as constructing a biblical pyramid. The capstone will be a methodological one; however, it is impossible to suspend it on a sky hook. It must sit firmly on bases built from the ground up. Sort of like this:

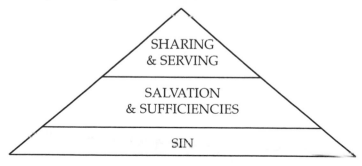

For the sake of organization, I will make each one of these levels a main stage of this building project (i.e. a division or part of this book). As we endeavor to build this pyramid, let me remind each construction-crew member to "be careful how he builds" (1 Corinthians 3:10b, taken slightly out of context, but not without applicational relevance).

Now just before we pour the massive biblical footing and foundation in Part I, permit me, as construction foreman, to say a word about who should be helping out on this project. Well, in final analysis, every genuine disciple of our Lord Jesus Christ needs to lend a hand. Although the biblical principles that our project will exhibit may be of the greatest benefit to vocational Bible teachers, apologists, pastors and the like because they are in "full-time ministries," the practicality of these precedents needs to grip every Christian. Whether you are an evangelist or share the Good News periodically when opportunities arise, whether you are a biblical counselor or sometimes communicate God's wisdom to needy members of the Body, whether you teach in a seminary or at times pass along God's Word more informally to people of all ages, etc., the "stuff" of these scriptural investigations is for all of us. The time is overdue *to do God's business His way* and not our own way.

Part I
SIN

Chapter 1
Total Depravity

If a physician hastily prescribes medicine without a thorough examination of the patient, without a diagnosis based upon the facts of his physical condition, he is setting himself up for a malpractice suit. How much more culpable is the Christian 'medic' who does not pay due regard to what the Bible says about man and sin! A superficial diagnosis in this most crucial realm bears eternal, not just temporal and physical, consequences. For example, unsaved people need a New-Covenant 'heart transplant.' If any of us should look upon unregenerate people as sick to some degree but not as being terminally ill and if we should come to them with a box of spiritual Band-Aids, this accomplishes nothing except possibly to place them at a higher level of accountability in the presence of our holy God. Furthermore, such possibly well-meaning, but theologically errant, medics will also stand before the judgment seat of Christ guilty of *spiritual* malpractice.

In this chapter on original sin and total depravity and the ones immediately following it, the Scriptures will paint a clear and sobering picture of man's innate sinfulness and his consequent inability 'to heal' himself (i.e. to save, himself). It will also become obvious that saved people still have a sin hangover that negatively affects some very practical areas of their lives. Therefore, *in and of ourselves,* we are incapable of sanctifying ourselves (cf., e.g., Galatians 3:3). Furthermore, although all Christian servants, be they 'professional' or not, are genuinely responsible to minister on all fronts in various ways, we must understand that we are but impotent medics on a great battlefield of spiritual carnage. This important recognition of our own helplessness should drive us to God's efficient provisions. Then and only then will we find ourselves in a humbled position *to do God's business His way.*

With this larger panorama in mind, let's go back and sketch out what the Bible says about the mutiny of mankind. As a reminder, I will begin more generally with original sin and total depravity and then gradually focus more specifically on the methodological significance of these biblical truths.

Man's Polluted 'Roots'

The Reality of the Fall

The facts of the Fall are chronicled in the Book of Genesis, chapters two and three. This is the story of Adam's terrible lapse. Preliminarily, I need to remind you that the Hebrew word for "Adam" is *a\da\m.* This term does indeed refer to "Adam," the first man, but it also denotes a "man" or "man" collectively as mankind. Sometimes, in certain contexts, these usages overlap. Therefore, this earliest of all references to Adam as the original 'father' of humankind, sets up an important relationship between what the Bible goes on to teach about 'the one' (i.e. Adam) and 'the many' (i.e. the human race traced back to him).

By clear implication, Adam was created "very good" according to God's pronouncement (cf. Genesis 1:26-31). It would seem reasonable that this divine assessment included an ethical evaluation of the first man and his wife Eve whose mediate creation is described in Genesis 2:18-25. Systematic theologians often label the first couple's original state as "untested" or "unconfirmed creaturely holiness." The first part of Ecclesiastes 7:29 memorializes the original condition of Adam and Eve when it says, "This only have I found: *God made mankind upright*, but men have gone in search of many schemes" (NIV, emphasis added).

Mankind's test was to obey God, and the test-case involved only one tree in a very lush and productive gar-

den. God's command was exceedingly clear. Let me paraphrase the Hebrew text of Genesis 2:17 like this: "But
contrastingly [i.e. in contrast with all the other trees with
their great cornucopia of produce given to the original
pair, i.e. v.16] from the tree of the knowledge of both
good and evil you must not (or, don't; or, never) eat from
it, because on the day you eat from it, you are surely (or,
indeed; or, truly) going to die." It is futile to try to ease
Adam's culpability by arguing that the reason part of this
command did not register with him since he had no experience with death of any kind as yet. From the force of
God's command, he had to have known that this was a
very serious divine demand the breaking of which would
bring with it catastrophic consequences. By the way, because of the clarity and specificity of God's command,
when Adam disobeyed it, he not only "sinned" (i.e. generally missed God's moral mark), but more high-handed-
ly, he "transgressed" an explicit divine injunction. He
stepped over an exceedingly well-marked line the LORD
Himself had drawn (i.e. Genesis 2:17; cf. the teaching of
Romans 5:13-14, 20 on how explicit law or command
turns "sin," in general, into specific "transgression").

At the outset of Genesis 3 *Satan's* serpent (cf. Genesis
3:14-15 with Romans 16:20) enters the picture. He first
majors on the minor raising doubts in Eve's mind about
the goodness of God (v. 1). Then after her summary and
supplement of God's original command of Genesis 2:17,
that "ancient serpent" (cf., e.g., Revelation 12:9) outright-
ly denied what the Lord had said. Let me paraphrase his
words: "There is no way that you are really going to die."
Finally, this crafty critter impugns God, serving up to Eve
the half-truth (i.e. the half-lie) recorded in verse 5. It was
true that their eyes would be opened; however, they
would painfully come to know evil by a catastrophic experience. He had hidden the infinitely high price tag of
such disobedience from her.

His malignant mission was successful as verse 6 indicates. She ate, gave also to her husband, and thereby they

fell from a state of being good into one plagued by guilt (i.e. vv. 7ff.). Spiritual death (death at its core involves separation) immediately occurred and it would be followed by physical death (cf. Genesis 3:19 with the 'obituary column' of chapter 5).

This story of Adam and Eve is also bad news for the whole race that would come from this original couple. There are many important solidarities bottled up in the last part of the curse pronounced by God upon the satanic serpent (i.e. v. 15). However, by the inexplicable grace of God, there is also hope therein for mankind. No wonder that traditionally Genesis 3:15 has been dubbed the *protoevangelium* (i.e. the first preaching of the Gospel). From here we could well move on to Romans 16:20, Galatians 3:16, etc., but that would be getting ahead of ourselves. Remember, we must detain an investigation of God's great salvation until we get a biblical picture of man in sin.

Let's continue painting this scriptural portrait of the race by turning to Romans 5:12-19. In this passage the interrelationship of the offense of the one (i.e. Adam) and the sin of the many (i.e. the human race) is discussed quite extensively. Consequently, these verses interpret the fact of the Fall with an emphasis on its implications for all humankind.

Since I cannot indulge in all the details of this passage which overflows with theological significance, it is wise to begin by offering a few keys to an understanding of it. At its core it speaks of two "men" (i.e. the first man, Adam, and the second or last man, Christ), their two contrasting acts (i.e. the disobedience of the first man and the obedience of the "last Adam"), and finally the significance of each of their acts for their respective constituencies.

The phenomenon that each of these men were corporate representatives and that their respective constituencies (i.e. the people they theologically represent) stand in union or solidarity, both with them and the consequences of their respective acts, is supported by many pieces of data from this text of Scripture. For example, one should carefully study this passage noting the following: 1) the little 'channel' preposition *dia,* usually translated "through" (cf., e.g., v. 12a, v. 12b, v. 16a, v. 17a, v. 17b, v. 18a, v. 18b, v. 19a, v. 19b); 2) other statements about the *means* of each of the representative's legacies being passed along to the many (cf., e.g., *"by means of* the transgression of the one" versus *"by means of* the grace of the one man, Jesus Christ" in v. 15; *"by means of* the transgression of the one" in v. 17a); 3) the result or outcome preposition *eis,* literally translated "unto" (cf., e.g., "so death spread *unto* all men" in v. 12b; "the gift . . . abounds (i.e. overflows) *unto* the many" in v. 15b; "on the one hand the judgment [literally ➔] *out of* one *unto* condemnation, but on the other hand the grace-gift . . . *unto* justification" in v. 16b; ". . . *unto* all men *unto* condemnation" versus ". . . *unto* all men *unto* justification of life" in v. 18); 4) the fact that the "consequently then" or "so then" at the head of v. 18 grammatically completes the comparison introduced in v. 12; and 5) the significance of the forensic (legal) background of the two occurrences of the Greek verb *kathistēmi* in v. 19 (i.e. "for just as through the disobedience of the one man the many *were* (judicially) *constituted* sinners, so also through the obedience of the one the many *were constituted* righteous ones"). So through many analogies and parallelisms, the respective parties of mankind are reckoned to be in solidarity with their respective principals. All people stand in a solidarity or union of fallenness with Adam; however, those out of them "who receive the abundance of grace and of the gift of righteousness" (Romans 5:17, NASB) stand in a 'saved' solidarity "in Christ."

But for right now, let's place the overwhelming truths about our solidarity with Christ and the salvation it brings on the 'back burner.' This union with Christ is another example of the amazing grace of God in salvation that will be the focal point of part two of our theological/ methodological journey. So, looking back on the dark side of the equation from Romans 5:12ff., it informs us that Adam *became* a sinner when he transgressed God's explicit commandment. But we are born sinners because of our union with him. We do not become sinners with our first disobedient thought or action; we are born sinners. We are fully responsible for our own sins (cf. the very last clause of Romans 5:12, "because all have sinned" with the condemning evidences of Romans 1:18ff. discussed below); nevertheless, the 'inheritance' of our culpability traces back to our 'great, great, great, . . . grand daddy' Adam. Building upon this theological 'footing' we need to construct a foundation upon it.

The Results of the Fall

Two representative passages out of many will help to bridge the experiential gap from the one to the many. The consequences of the Fall were not only catastrophic for Adam but also for us.

Let's listen first to David's personal testimony in Psalm 51:5. Although not every human being has committed adultery and murdered another person's spouse, the wicked potentialities of our fallen nature, unchecked by the grace of God, are unbounded. The principles that David deeply meditates upon in Psalm 51:5 stand behind all manifestations of humankind's actual sins whatever variety they may be.

The first four verses of the psalm set the stage for the affirmations of verse 5. We must not assume from an isolated and superficial examination of v. 5 that David is claiming to have been 'victimized.' He is not 'passing the buck' to his mother or to Adam or to whomever, so as to exonerate himself. His penitential prayers of vv. 1-4 clearly indicate that he is taking full responsibility for his heinous actions. What he is doing however in v. 5 is plumbing the dark depths of his being to try to understand better the cesspool out of which such abominable deeds had arisen.

Verse 5 contains two parallel lines of Hebrew poetry (remember that one of the beauties of Hebrew poetry is that its parallelisms are logical, thereby they convey their impact through any adequate translation). Herein the lines are synonymously related, although the second member gets down even deeper beneath sin's surface deeds. In other words, David in v. 5a speaks of his sinful state at parturation from the womb (i.e. at birth), while in v. 5b he antedates it by nine months speaking about his condition at the moment of his conception.

Psalm 51:5a (v. 7a in the Hebrew text) reads: "Behold, in iniquity [cf. his personally owned "iniquity" in v. 2a] I was brought forth." A vivid picture of childbirth is conveyed by the imagery of this verb "to bring forth." A woman is pictured as writhing or twisting in labor pains until her child is born. Here David stresses the fact that when he was born, it was into a condition of ethical twistedness, i.e. into an estate of moral perversity. When the midwife slapped his hind parts, and he took his first breath of air, he had a 'bent' [pun on the Hebrew word intended] to deviate from what is holy and right. The images of v. 5a are similar to those employed in the description of "the wicked" in Psalm 58:3.

Furthermore, as he goes deeper into the muck of his meanness, he sadly testifies to the fact that "in sin my mother conceived me" (v. 5b.). His condition at conception could be described as one of missing God's moral mark (cf. the literal background of this important Hebrew root "to miss" in Judges 20:16). When sperm and egg come together in the procreation of a person, that new being is already in a state of moral failure. The roots of our depravity indeed are exceedingly deep.

Now let's jump to a crucially significant New Testament passage, Ephesians 2:1, 3. I'm going to detain our investigation into the contribution of v. 2 until the topic of satanic opposition comes up later. And I'm also going to put off, temporarily, a consideration of Ephesians 2:4ff., a great "BUT GOD" passage about His sovereignty in salvation, except to note here that the grammatical objects of His great love and grace are brought forward into vv. 1-3 of Ephesians 2 as the sinful subjects of His unfathomable mercy. Consequently, we find in this chapter a typically biblical 'before' and 'after' contrast, that is our B. C. existence (our spiritually bankrupt condition prior to the application of the Person and work of Christ to our account) is starkly contrasted with our A. C. existence (our after-Christ-and-His-crosswork life which God has mercifully granted to us).

The universality of the depravity sketched out by Paul in Ephesians 2:1, 3 is inescapably obvious. Compare especially the "you" at the outset of v.1 [i.e. the audience of professing believers at Ephesus], the "also all of us" at the beginning of v. 3 [i.e. Paul and his companions join the crowd], and the "as even the rest" at the end of v. 3, referring to all "disobedient sons" (v. 2), all "children" deserving of "wrath" (v. 3). This theological sieve is so fine that no human being can slip through it.

Now what does Paul say about all people apart from Christ and His cross? Literally this: "You being dead people in connection with (or, possibly, "because of") your transgressions and sins, . . . we all previously lived (i.e. conducted our lives) in the lusts of our flesh, doing the desires of the flesh and of our (literally, "the") minds, and we were by nature children of wrath as also the rest" (Ephesians 2:1, 3). By the way, notice the common scriptural vehicle of expressing the interrelationship of being and doing: v. 1 speaks of 'being'; vv. 2-3a emphasize 'doing'; and v. 3b returns to the 'being' that underlies the 'doing.'

For right now, concentrate on the 'being.' The participle of v. 1 utilizes the most common state of being verb in Greek, and its present tense speaks of our consistently characterizing condition in the past. We were in a state of deadness. Our offenses and moral failures *separated* us from the Lord (remember the original consequences for Adam when he violated God's command). Furthermore, since we were dead, in and of ourselves we were totally unresponsive to God and the things of God. We were alive biologically, but spiritually we were as dead as proverbial "door nails."

Verse 3 adds its weight to this helpless and hopeless condition; all trophies of God's grace were formerly "children of wrath *by nature*," i.e. we were such innately or naturally, not by apprenticeship nor by any other after-the-fact means. This is the gist of original sin and total depravity. Need I say that these truths carry along with them overwhelming, methodological significance. We must understand that since all people are depraved by nature and are spiritually dead, they do not and cannot rescue themselves from eternal disaster, nor can anyone save them by employing the mere methods of men. Much more about this awesome theological-methodological reality later.

As I continue to build on this solid footing and foundation, I am amazed at not only how so many people disregard or minimize these truths about man's polluted 'roots,' but how they also turn a deaf ear to another mass of scriptural evidence. The Bible from cover to cover publishes headlines not about the goodness of man, but about his malignant history. Indeed, many proverbs or proverbial-like affirmations about man in his fallen estate dot the pages of Scripture.

Man's Profane Reputation

The scriptural evidences for man's bad 'rep' are so vast that it calls for much editorial activity in the 'cutting out' of some of the most scandalous, biblical headlines. I'll try to get a good sampling of various speakers or writers.

It seems best to begin with some testimonies which possibly come from the most ancient book of the Bible. If Job is not the oldest book [i.e. at least as regarded so by most conservative scholars], it preserves ancient traditions and teachings. Its selected maxims coming from the mouths of Job, Eliphaz, Bildad, and Zophar needed time to have been recognized and accepted as proverbial 'tidbits.' Since these were theological axioms apparently recognized by both sides of this extended dialogue, it is not necessary to get into some of the heavy hermeneutics (i.e. the interpretive principles and guidelines) needed to handle this particular book of the Bible accurately. The bottom line for my appeal to such traditionally canonized statements about fallen man is their mutual acceptability. These sweeping generalizations were looked upon as being accurate reflections on the reputation of man.

Eliphaz, in Job 4:17, uses synonymous rhetorical questions supposedly to bolster his accusation against Job, saying: "Can mankind be just before God? Can a man be pure before his Maker?" (NASB; note that the alternative translation of the NIV does not fit well into this context). Very interestingly, of all the Hebrew words available for "man," two different ones lying on opposite connotational ends are employed here. The term in v. 17a could be nuanced 'puny' man, while the one in v. 17b would take on the coloring 'macho' man. The point is that it does not matter how you view mankind, whether in his weakness or his supposed strength, he has absolutely no claim to righteousness nor to moral cleanness, especially in the holy presence of his Creator-God. So Eliphaz's general aphorisms, his maxims about men, are true; however, his application of them to some assumed, *particular* sin of Job which had brought the judgments of God upon the patriarch was 'off base.'

Job asks, and answers, a similar rhetorical question in chapter 14, verse 4: "Who can bring what is pure from the impure? No one!" (NIV). The gist is that no human being is able to turn what is defiled into what is clean. Support for the application of this rhetorical question to the depraved condition of the whole race comes not only from the context of these various arguments which run through the book of Job but also from a host of passages such as 1 Kings 8:46; Psalm 130:3; Psalm 143:2; Proverbs 20:9; John 3:6; etc. Job intended his question to be applied to man in sin, and his terse answer ruled out any possibility of self- or social reform.

Eliphaz speaks again in Job 15:14-16 singing an old song in v. 14 with an added chorus of vv. 15-16. The old song (cf., Job 4:17ff; 9:2; 14:4; etc.) goes like this: "What is [puny] man, that he could be pure? Or one born of a woman that he could be just (or righteous)?" Now the new chorus on an old theme continues with these words of indictment: "Behold, He [i.e. the LORD] does not trust in His holy ones [i.e. holy angels in the context of Job], and the heavens are not pure in his eyes [i.e. in His absolutely holy assessment], how much less, one who is repulsive and abhorrent, man, who drinks perversity like water!" The statement about man being "born of woman" in the last part of v. 14 is likely a reference to a 'hereditary' connection to sin (cf. e.g., Psalm 51:5 again).

Verse 15 sets up the shocking comparison of verse 16 (i.e. "How much less"). By emphasizing the beings that live and minister in God's very presence and His heavenly dwelling place, and by affirming that they are not respectively trustworthy and pure, the punchline on humankind in v. 16 explodes with nuclear force. The explicit identification of the subject under consideration in v. 16, i.e. "man," is detained for added effect. Two descriptives come first. The first speaks of man as being "vile" (NIV) or "detestable." The force of this particular term in this particular context is ethically "repulsive." Then the second term comes alongside to reinforce this metaphor of moral malignancy. Man is further called "corrupt" (NASB; NIV; etc.) or "depraved" (cf. the RSV's rendering of this same term in Psalm 53:3). This exceedingly descriptive term, based on a root which in a related Semitic language describes sour milk, regards mankind as being spiritually repugnant and ethically abhorrent (cf. its other occurrences in Psalms 14:3 and 53:3 along with some discussion below).

Finally in the last line of Job 15:16 man is described by a characterizing activity, "he drinks iniquity, or perversity, or wickedness like water." This simile "like water" emphasizes that humankind gulps down any and every form of evil naturally, and continually, and 'by the gallon.'

In Job 25:4-6 Bildad joins the previous choruses with a slight illustrative variation in the last verse. Using old rhetorical questions in v. 4, he implies that all human beings are unrighteous and impure. Then in v. 5 he sets up yet another stark contrast with the wickedness of humanity by arguing that even the heavenly bodies are not bright and clean according to the evaluation of the thrice holy God. This shocking truth about the creation on high then drops to the lowest recesses of the earthly domain below: "how much less [puny] man, a maggot, and a son of man [i.e. *ben ādām* in Hebrew], a worm!" (v. 6). The phrase "son of *ādām*" is a common Semitic way of referring to mankind. It is likely that this phrase conveys a sameness of nature with their fallen father "Adam." Nevertheless, biblically the phrase most often emphasizes humanity's finiteness and/or fallenness. The creatures chosen to represent man are indeed the lowliest of the lowly. First, there is the "maggot" which is associated with rottenness and decay. Interestingly, the early Greek translation of the Old Testament called the Septuagint (LXX), uses the term "decay" for this "maggot." A member of this same Greek word-group shows up in our Lord's picture of certain unrighteous people; they are described by Him as "*rotten* trees" (cf., e.g., Matthew 7:17ff.; 12:33; etc.). So man as a "maggot" is putrid, not pure.

Secondly, Bildad's proverb labels humanity a "worm." This word is associated with what is abominable, detestable, or offensive. Consequently, man is depicted ethically as having a foul subterrestrial nature. By the way, for a specific example of one especially blasphemously arrogant man associated with maggots and worms compare the king of Babylon in Isaiah 14:11. Today it is tragic that the Bible's 'worm-theology' is being challenged and denied by the hermeneutics of humanism.

From these proverbial descriptions of man from Job, we are beginning to see how terrible the reputation of humanity really is. He is depicted as spiritually 'rotten to the core.' And as we continue our investigation, we're going to find out that his "core" is also rotten.

Let's listen to another testimony from David. In Psalm 14:1-3 (cf. the nearly identical parallel in Psalm 53:1-3) he says this about the fallen race (my expanded translation and paraphrase): "The fool [not a mental, but a moral, moron] says in his heart [i.e. in the core of his being; 'he says to himself'], 'There is no God' [i.e. practically, God does not exist as far as he is concerned]. They are corrupt (or perverse); they make abominable (their) deeds" [i.e. they do vile and horrible things]. There is not one doing good. The LORD looks down from heaven upon the sons of mankind (*ben ādām* again; i.e. upon all humanity) to see if there is one [i.e. *any*one] who understands [i.e. who acts wisely or prudently in all the practical issues of life], one [i.e. again, *any*one] who is seeking (or pursuing after) God. All [i.e. the whole lot of them] have turned aside (or departed) [i.e. all humanity has apostatized]; altogether [i.e. in union or solidarity] they have become corrupt [i.e. ethically putrefied, or morally rancid; cf. Job 15:16 again for this imagery]. There is not one doing good; not even one." Since the impact of these verses is so transparent, I will not comment further on this passage for now. Later, however, when it is quoted by Paul in Romans 3:10-12, we will return to these divine indictments of the race.

Next let's move from a sampling of what David says about the rancid reputation of humanity to a few corroborations of it coming to us through his son Solomon. This "wisest" of men comprehensively said this of the sinful race in 1 Kings 8:46: "for there is no man who does not sin" (NASB). Or phrasing his affirmation another way, "a human being who does not sin does not exist."

Now with this as background, listen to a few more of his assessments contained in Ecclesiastes. And again, as in the case of the Book of Job, it is not necessary to get into an in-depth study of the special hermeneutical principles pertaining to the interpretive challenges of Ecclesiastes. The bytes that I will be excerpting are not merely the opinions of a '"man under the sun,"' but they are accurate aphorisms about mankind as borne out by the analogy of all Scripture.

Ecclesiastes 7:20 is very similar to 1 Kings 8:46 in that it reaffirms, "Indeed, there is not a righteous man on earth who *continually* does good and who never sins" (NASB). This obviously is a dictum about depravity.

Earlier in discussing the untested creaturely holiness of Adam, I referred to Ecclesiastes 7:29a. Now it's time to place its antithetical line alongside of it: "This only I have found by observation, that God made mankind upright (or, straightforward, or, just), but they have sought out many devices" (or schemes; i.e. multiplied perverse plans). Instead of being ethically straight, after the Fall humanity is characterized as morally crooked in their thinkings and plannings.

In the middle of verse 3 of chapter 9, Solomon adds, "Moreover, the heart [the singular possibly implies the race's unified disposition] of the sons of man [i.e., men, humanity] are full of evil, and insanities (or, madnesses [i.e. masses of *moral* madness]) are in their heart as long as they live" (literally, throughout their lives). So the paintings that Solomon produces of man in sin join the huge scriptural gallery of humankind's grotesque portrait.

Before leaving the Old Testament, we must spend some time in the 17th chapter of Jeremiah. The structure of Jeremiah 17:5-8 is captivating, and its theological contents are overwhelming. Based upon the cursing and blessing formulas of the Old Testament (and the Ancient Near East), these verses fall into two stanzas, the cursed man of vv. 5-6 stands in a radical contrast with the blessed man of vv. 7-8. Furthermore, each portion unfolds in a similar manner: 1) the pronounced curse or blessing; 2) some crucial descriptions of the representative objects of either cursing or blessing, followed by 3) pertinent illustrations of these two broad categories of mankind. The subjects of these stanzas represent the two main divisions of mankind, i.e. the unrighteous and the righteous, the unregenerate and the regenerate, the lost and the saved, the humanist and the theist, etc. There are many echoes from the Psalms in these verses (cf. esp. Psalm 1).

Obviously, since we are dealing with humanity apart from the interventions of divine grace, I'll be concentrating on the cursed man. It must be noted that all of these assessments come from God Himself through His mouthpiece Jeremiah (i.e. "Thus says the LORD"). The (macho) man upon whom God pronounces His curse is one who is characterized by trusting in mankind [i.e. *ādām*]. It is quite interesting that the lead-off term for "man" both here and in v. 7 (i.e. there in reference to the "blessed man") connotes man in his supposed strength or prowess. Also, the term for "trusting" plus the little preposition "in" following it are identical in both cases. The combination indicates what a person puts his confidence in, what he believes in, etc. Concerning the blessed man of v. 7, he is characterized by trusting in Yahweh, and furthermore his object of confidence (i.e. a noun form from this same important word group) is the LORD Himself. Not so, the cursed humanist; he trusts in mankind. Faith in humankind, whether it is in oneself or ones allies (cf. the larger context) is bound to disaster, especially since God has made it clear throughout His word that *ādām* is both finite and fallible. Furthermore, it is said of this foolish fellow that "he makes flesh [another term often used to designate humanity, and again as limited and insufficient] his arm" [i.e. an image for his resource or strength]. The last description of the self-deceived believer in humanity is one that characterizes him as apostate, i.e. "his heart [i.e. his mission-control center; cf. below on Jeremiah 17:9] departs (or, turns away) from the LORD." No wonder this representative of all of fallen humanity is depicted as an undesirable piece of sage brush in the desert (v. 6) in radical contrast with the tree-in-an-oasis picture of the divinely blessed believer (v. 8).

Immediately following this poetic unit are the universally applicable affirmations about all people in their natural estate (including those who mercifully are being rescued out of their pitiful plight). God now focuses His spiritual MRI on mankind's core of being. His infallible diagnosis is written up like this: "The heart [of man] is more treacherous (or, deceitful; or, crafty) than all [i.e. than anything there is] and desperately sick."

The human "heart" (Hebrew, *lēb* or *lēbab*; Greek, *kardia*), being biblically the center of man's conscience existence, is a most comprehensive anthropological term. Its primary functions include thinking, willing, and planning. As we are going to see shortly from Genesis 6:5 and other passages, such scriptural 'givens' about mankind's "heart" carry with them tons of methodological freight. Here in Jeremiah 17:9 we find a comprehensive statement about humankind's spiritual 'heart trouble.' Using the superlative degree, the LORD pronounces the human heart more insidious than anything and everything one could possibly nominate as an alternative candidate. The descriptive adjective used here derives from a verb that means "to deal treacherously." The root of this term also shows up in the personal name "Jacob," and we all know of his capability when it came to conniving. Indeed, here in Jeremiah, the whole race is divinely diagnosed with a conniving, crafty, deceitful core of being.

Furthermore, by using a contrasting word-picture with the (macho) "man" references found back in verses 5 and 7, man's heart is now further described as being "weak" or "sick." This adjective comes from the same word-group from which the noun (*puny*) "man" derives. The truth that humanity's "heart" is spiritually sick reinforces again the major teaching about man's finiteness and falleness. As a matter of fact, we're so sick and weak by nature that we cannot come up with an anywhere-near-accurate self diagnosis. The words at the very end of v. 9, "who can understand it," confirm this sad situation. And indeed, if we can't fully understand our potentially fatal spiritual disease, how can we, with our bankrupt resources, cure ourselves or any one else? Consequently, if fallen man is to live spiritually, God must implant in him a new heart based upon His *perfect* diagnostic insights (cf. v. 10).

Moving from the Old Testament into the New Testament, avalanches of data could be put forth to support man's profane reputation. I'm going to appeal to only three texts out of many that preserve our Lord's estimations of the ethical perversities of all mankind. The first two verses selected say essentially the same thing; however, contextually these proverbial characterizations are applied by Christ, first to the hypocritical religious leaders of His day and then to His own disciples. Noteworthy in each case is the fact that none from these respective audiences contested these assessments, not one arrogant Pharisee nor the impetuous Peter for example. Our Lord said this in Matthew 12:34a (concentrate on my italicized flaggings of these universal 'givens'): "You brood of vipers, how can you, *being evil* [i.e. continually characterized as being evil people] speak good things?" His point is that because they were innately evil, it was impossible for them to speak good. They had no ability in themselves as fallen men to consistently communicate good things.

Now turning to His disciples, Jesus says this in Luke 11:13 a: "If you then, *being evil* [i.e. continually and characteristically existing as evil people], know to give good gifts to your children, . . ." So, the root of evil in man, whether lost or saved, is not easily eradicated. It calls for the initiative and continuing interventions of a merciful God.

One of the clearest and most significant passages on the very bad 'rep' of humanity is found in Mark 7 (cf. also the parallel in Matthew 15). In the seventh chapter of Mark a controversy was kindled by the religious externalists of Jesus' day. They taught that men became unclean from the outside in; therefore, they zealously promoted all kinds of ritual 'cleansings.' Jesus first told the crowd publicly and then His own disciples privately that such teachings had turned God's revelation upside down (the repeated and extended explanations to His own disciples demonstrated how deeply ingrained this false conception was). So by these repetitions and by careful theological reasonings Jesus set out to correct this wrong thinking about the source of mankind's defilement.

Let me begin with Christ's correction in vv. 14b-15. Jesus said to the crowd: '"Listen to Me, everyone, and understand this. Nothing outside a man can make him 'unclean' by going into him. Rather, it is what comes out of a man that makes him 'unclean'"' (NIV). Note that the contrast in conceptions (i.e. between their false conception and Jesus' biblical conception) is perpetuated throughout this passage (cf., e.g., "outside . . . going into" man versus what "comes out of" him here in v. 15; and "going into" man "from the outside" in v. 18 versus what "goes out of" man in v. 20; and "from within, out of the heart" of man in v. 21). Man's spiritual pollution does not originate from the *outside* but from the *inside*. With this in mind, permit me to translate very literally at times and also to paraphrase at times Jesus' punch-line in vv. 20-23: "Now he kept on saying, 'That which goes out from, out of the man himself indeed that defiles (or, pollutes; or, makes unclean) the man; for from within, out of the fountainhead of the heart of men emanate bad thinking processes, fornications, thefts, murders, adulteries, covetings, evil things, deceit, lewdness, an evil eye, blasphemy, arrogance, foolishness; all of these evil things come from within and defile the man.'" The list of sins in vv. 21-22 is not exhaustive. It is ethically representative of attitudes and activities condemned by God in His Word. The main issue is that all of such kinds of wickedness come out of the core of man's being, his depraved heart. His mission-control center is notorious for what it generates. Especially, pay careful attention to what lies at the head of the list, i.e. "bad thoughts"; or, "evil schemings"; or, "wicked designs." This emphasis on man's mental perversity excellently sets the stage for his wickedly twisted thinking dealt with in the following section.

But before we go there, I'd like to ask the question "How did this perfect insight into the insidious heart of man affect Jesus' ministerial methodology?" Well, I think we can find an answer to this important question in John 2:23-25: "Now while he [i.e. Christ] was in Jerusalem at the Passover Feast, many people saw the miraculous signs he was doing and believed in his name. But Jesus would not entrust himself to them [literally, taking off on the previous reference to their 'believing,' "He did not believe them"], for he knew all men. He did not need man's testimony about man, for he knew what was in man" (NIV). And what was in man? A desperately wicked heart. Therefore, He always kept this truth in mind and thereby consistently carried on *God's business God's way*. Would that we heed His example when it comes to accepting fully what God's Word says about the profane reputation of fallen humanity.

Man's Perverted Reasoning

The importance of the noetic [from the Greek word *nous*, "mind," i.e. *mental*] effects of the Fall cannot be overestimated. Tragically, they have been ignored or underestimated even by many ministers who claim to hold firmly to the doctrines of grace. Consequently, fallen man has been wrongly regarded as having an ability to 'think through' eternal and spiritual issues without significant hindrance. While his mental faculties may function perfectly in the areas of math and other non-moral disciplines [i.e. 2+2 will equal 4], they are thoroughly skewed when it comes to understanding spiritual things [i.e. for the autonomous, unregenerate person who locks God out of his sphere of supposed reality, 2+2 will equal 3 or 5 every time he is confronted with spiritual things]. It takes the efficacies of God to change his mind [i.e. repentance] and world-and-life view and also to progressively transform his mind according to the "mind of Christ" [i.e. renewal]. But we're getting ahead of ourselves again. For right now, it is necessary to understand biblically the spiritually radical dysfunction of fallen man's mind.

Once again, the choice of only two sample texts does not indicate the data are scarce. Explicit and implicit indications of noetic depravity salt and pepper both the Old and the New Testament Scriptures. The two passages I have chosen, however, are especially clear on this most vital point of hamartiology [i.e. the doctrine of sin].

The terrorizing truth of Genesis 6:5 comes full strength since it is condensed into just a few weighted words in the Hebrew text. Just before I offer you my translation and interpretive rendering of it, a word about the context is in order. The first thirteen verses of Genesis 6 exemplify the accelerating corruption of mankind upon the earth as a background to the great flood judgment. The "man," "flesh," and "all flesh" designations of verse 5 and 11-12 speak of the totality of fallen humanity. Humankind was rapidly rising up in moral mutiny. In the midst of this historical chronicle is placed the two divine assessments of v. 5.

As the LORD scrutinized the race's accelerating anarchy, He paid careful attention to its breadth (v. 5a) and its depth (v. 5b). Consequently, besides the importance of the noetic significance of Genesis 6:5b, the whole verse illustrates what *total* depravity means. It is universal in its corporate scope, and it is individually deep-seated in its internal devastations.

When it says that "the LORD saw that the evil (or, wickedness) of man [i.e. mankind] was great on earth," He was summarizing innumerable manifestations of moral mutiny. As He looked across the horizons of the planet, he observed human rebellion out of control. It was pandemic.

Then, like Jesus would do on another occasion in future human history (cf. Mark 7 above), Yahweh here identified the source of every kind of expression of wickedness, i.e. the human heart. However, in Genesis 6:5 the LORD particularly points to the fallen heart's noetic dysfunction. With His MRI eyes, He saw "that every inclination of the thoughts of his heart was only evil all the time" (v. 5b, NIV). The Hebrew text begins with a chain of words linked together [i.e. a construct chain]. At the end of the line [i.e. the absolute form] is the human heart out of which the previous functions emanate. So the subject of our LORD's scrutiny taken as a bound unit was "each and every intention [i.e. better *formulation*; this Hebrew word-group conveys images of a potter] of the thoughts [i.e. mankind's thinking processes] of the heart" [i.e. that core of being that pilots the whole course of ones life]. So what God is especially x-raying are the thinking and planning functions of the human heart.

What is His evaluation based upon this divine examination? It is that the controlling core of man's life is "only evil continually" (NASB). In other words, it is *exclusively* and *continually* "bad," "evil," or "wicked." Consequently, man's thinking and reasoning processes are consistently depraved in reference to the vital moral issues of life because of the race's spiritual heart disease. Not so incidentally, the '*be*-graced' Noah and his family were not exempt from this diagnosis of depravity (cf. Genesis 8:21).

Ephesians 4:17-19 is another exceedingly relevant text when it comes to the ravages of noetic depravity. Contextually, it falls in the second half of this epistle of Paul which focuses on the believer's walk [i.e. life-style and conduct]. Notice how this mega-topic is introduced in Ephesians 4:1 and then picked up and fully expanded in 4:17ff. Consequently, the interrelationship of 'being' and 'doing' found in Ephesians 4:17-19 sets the stage for the many ethical exhortations contained in the remainder of this epistle. Technically, the interrelationship that Paul highlights is more specifically one of 'thinking' and 'doing.' Not only is 'as a man *is*, so he does' a biblical truism, but so also is 'as a man *thinks*, so he does.'

With great urgency and intensity Paul writes: "This therefore I say and testify to [cf. the NIV's "insist on"] in the Lord, that you no longer walk [either 'stop,' or 'no longer have the habit of living'] just as even the Gentiles [herein, non-Christians, unbelievers] walk [i.e. carry on their lives], in the futility (or, vanity; or, emptiness; or, purposelessness) of their mind [i.e. *nous*], people characterized as being in a darkened condition in reference to their understanding [i.e. emphasizing the functioning of their mind faculties], ones alienated [i.e. resultantly separated] from the life of God, on account of the [culpable] ignorance which is in them [i.e. innately], on account of the hardness [i.e. their morally impervious callused condition] of their heart; which many people, having become insensitive, have given themselves over to sensuality unto the practicing of every kind of impurity with an insatiable lust" (Ephesians 4:17-19). What Paul says in vv. 17-18 about the depraved "heart" and "mind" of 'the many,' he also emphasized in a condensed form in Romans 1:21, and therein a subtle connection is drawn between the condition of 'the many' and the lapse of the original 'one.' A discussion of that passage is forthcoming (cf. below).

Returning to Ephesians 4 and our special focus on noetic depravity, it is important to stress how the *nous*, the "mind" of man apart from a merciful divine intervention, is utterly futile when it comes to living a life pleasing to God. Unregenerate people are incapable of doing anything good since they are in a darkened condition in reference to their spiritual understanding. Once again, we see that the ravages of human depravity negatively effect not just the will of man, according to the restricted view of some, but also and especially his mental functions in application to the issues that really count for life and for eternity.

Man's Perpetual Resistance

The whole Bible and all history document this terrible reality; therefore, the following treatment once again must be representative and synthetic. The following examples will illustrate this general theme of perpetual resistance, manifesting itself both through man's flight from God and his active hostility towards his Creator.

An Inspired History: Romans 1:18-32

These verses fully apply to the fallen race; however, by intimation, they also trace back to "the beginning" and the seminal sin of Adam and Eve (cf., e.g., v. 21). Waters from the Genesis account of the Fall bathe these lines of Paul as he begins to build his case for the universal condemnation of all humanity, whether people be of Jewish or of Gentile ethnic heritage.

Paul cites many explicit sins in vv. 24ff. In three choruses, based upon mankind's resistance and rejection of their Creator-Lord, Paul says, "God gave (or, delivered) them over to . . ." (vv. 24ff., 26ff., 28ff.). Notice especially how the first and third choruses launch out: "God delivered them over in connection with the lusts of their hearts to . . ." (v. 24) and "God delivered them over to a depraved mind, to practice . . ." (v. 28). This biblical picture is consistent; all deeds, here samples of vile practices, emanate out of the human "heart" and "mind." God's judicial 'deliverings-over' could be expressed more personally like this: "Okay, you rebellious resistors, you want it; you got it!"

The thing I want to dwell on in this passage is epistemology [i.e. the study of knowledge], particularly focusing on its biblical applications and limitations. Many throughout the annals of church history have assumed that Paul in Romans 1:18ff. is arguing that the evidences of God's handiwork in His creation have the power to break through human hardness [i.e., man by examining these evidences can come to a *true* knowledge of the *true* God].

That the creation does bear a real witness, both externally and internally, to man about God is indeed taught in this passage (cf. vv. 19-20a). However, in his autonomous, persistent resistance to this truth, with every dogged breath of his being, man refuses to let this "'knowledge'" take root in him spiritually. Verse 18 is clear on this: "For the wrath of God is being revealed from heaven against all the ungodliness and unrighteousness of men who are suppressing (i.e. habitually holding down and hindering) the truth in unrighteousness." Fallen humanity is characterized by their consistent suppression of the truth about God, herein especially as it is clearly manifested in the creation. The present, descriptive participle "suppressing" depicts the fallen race as ever and always keeping this truth about God incarcerated. For that reason, there is only one possible outcome; as Paul states it, "so that they [i.e. mankind] are without excuse" (i.e. without a defense). Interestingly, the Greek word he uses to expose their culpability is the word which comes into English as "apologetic" plus a negation glued on to the front of it [i.e. they have *no* apologetic]. They cannot defend themselves in the presence of the Creator who is now also pictured as their awesome Judge.

Needless to say, this passage speaks to the fact that the evidences of God manifested in nature cannot convert; they can only condemn because of mankind's universal and continuous rejection and resistance of God. However, the truth of this passage must also speak to the servants of

God, for example, informing them that the so-called "theistic arguments" have no power to save. Fallen man's autonomous world-and-life view will prohibit him from taking such reasonings seriously, no matter how carefully, skillfully, and eloquently they may be presented.

An Inspired Review: Romans 3:9-18

Romans 3:9-18 contains a chain of Old Testament quotations brought together by Paul. They function aggregately as the punch-line to his first major section of this grand epistle about the Gospel of God's sovereign grace. In this closing argument fourteen biblical indictments come together and lead to the divine verdict of the universal condemnation of the whole race. By the way, it is methodologically noteworthy that when Paul comes in with a *coupes de grace,* it usually involves his utilization of God's Word. Even though he, as an apostle, a proxy of Christ, had the authority of our Lord behind him, he nevertheless appealed to the authority of Scripture again and again as the final word (notice his introductory formula here in v. 10a, "it stands written" [i.e. it was inscripturated in the past but still carries full force with current applications]). How much more should we non-apostolic servants be characterized by such a reliance upon God's sufficient provisions from His Word.

The apostle's fourteen indictments which review the resistance of mankind may be grouped logically into four categories: 1) mankind's character, vv. 10-12; 2) his communications, vv. 13-14; 3) his conduct, vv. 15-17; and 4) his contempt, v. 18. Romans 3:10b-12 comes from Psalm 14:1-3 (cf. the discussion above, along with the parallel passage in Psalm 53:1-3; these truths must really be important – God repeated Himself at least three times!). The Greek text is substantively similar to the Hebrew. Paul's rendition goes like this: "There is not a righteous person, not even one; there is not one who understands [contextually, the thrust is no person has proper perception; i.e.

no one can correctly line things up in his mind when it comes to spiritual matters]; there is not one who seeks out God [the Bible again makes it very clear that the natural man will not and cannot seek God—What does this say about '"seeker services"'?]. All [men; or, people] have turned aside [i.e. *away from God]*, altogether they have become useless (or, worthless [i.e. depraved]); there is not one who does (or, practices) goodness, there is not even one."

Previously, we viewed God as the perfect spiritual Cardiologist; now in Romans 3:13-14 we see Him functioning as an infallible, EN*T* diagnostician (i.e. the Great Physician as an ears, nose, and *throat* specialist): "Their throat (literally, larynx) is an open grave; with their tongues they have habitually practiced deceit; the poison of vipers is under their lips, their mouth being full of cursing and bitterness." Their speech reveals the depraved nature of their heart. This biblical truth is found in all corners of the Old and New Testament. Heavily concentrated evidences of, and warnings about, man's malignant mouth may be observed throughout the Book of Proverbs. That portion of the Old Testament not only reveals his 'mouth' disease, it also deals extensively with his 'hoof' disease (i.e. the unethical pathways he regularly travels).

Such 'hoof' disease is Paul's next focus in Romans 3:15-17: "Their feet are swift to shed blood; destruction and misery are in their paths, and a way of peace they have not known." All humankind's meanderings are mean. All the circuits of their conduct bear the earmarks of hostility.

Finally, comes the 'mother' of all indictments. By implication, the horrible reality of v. 18 could be regarded as the bottom-line reason for all the previous exhibitions of the race's moral apostasy: "There is no fear of God before their eyes." We have come full circle to practical atheism. Such a basic attitude and outlook calls for divine 'dynamite' to remove it.

An Inspired Synthesis: Romans 5:6-10

At this juncture Romans 5:6-10 will be used to exemplify the hopelessness and helplessness of mankind left to himself. Later on, we will return to this message showing how God mercifully breaks through such resistances. Again, detaining what God does for the elect, let me put the spotlight on what we were like when God saved us. Obviously, this is another one of those B. C. and A. C. texts.

B. C. - wise, it first says in v. 6: "while (or, although) we were yet without strength" [i.e. spiritually, we were powerless and helpless]. Then in v. 8, with intensifying accountability, it affirms: "while (or, although) we were still sinners" [i.e. while we were yet in a characterizing condition of moral failure]. And finally, pointing to an even higher level of accountability, Paul places God's marvelous work of grace into this dismal setting: "while (or, although) we were enemies" [i.e. of God]. What Paul says here in v. 10 of Romans 5 is reinforced by similar affirmations in Colossians 1:21. The B. C. part of Colossians 1:21-23 literally reads: "and you formerly being alienated and enemies in the mind . . ." (v. 21a). When God reconciled us (v. 22), we were in an estate of alienation from Him, and furthermore, in reference to our minds, we were actively hostile towards Him. Notice how the words "enemies in the mind" interrelate both man's perverted reasoning and his perpetual resistance. All such biblical notations vividly expose our pitiful B. C. condition up to the time when the Lord mercifully rescued us.

Chapter 2
Total Inability
Primary Affirmations of It

Continuing my precedent of selective samplings, I have chosen two passages which sum up the pri-mary effect of total depravity, which is total inability. The first is found in Jeremiah 13:23 and is another example of rhetorical wisdom poetry. Its applicational punch line comes home like the fatal thrust of a sword. As the prophet continued to deal with the wayward majority in Judah, he said, "Can an Ethiopian [i.e. generally regarded as being dark skinned, no matter what the specific location of "Cush" may have been] change (i.e. turn; or, transform; or, alter) his skin (color) or the leopard his spots [e.g., into the tawny color of the coat of a lion]? (Then) even you would be able to do good who are accustomed to do evil" [interestingly, this last idiom comes from the discipleship word-group in Hebrew; if you will, Jeremiah looked upon his audience as *practiced disciples* in wickedness]. The NIV does a nice job of dynamically rendering the rhetorical structure of this verse, thereby exposing its central teaching: "Can the Ethiopian change his skin color or the leopard its spots? Neither can you do good who are accustomed to doing evil." The key thought is ability (really *in*ability); the Hebrew 'can-do' verb occurs in the second part of this verse (i.e. "*can*"; or, "*able* to do good"). Such hypothetical ability is utterly denied by the two sample scenarios in the first part of the verse. Since like begets like (an important and inviolable principle in nature and in Scripture; cf., e.g., John 3:6), it is impossible for those who are innately evil, as outwardly corroborated by their bad behavior, to practice good works. In and of themselves, they are unable to do so. So Jeremiah 13:23 is a good theological example of total inability.

Probably the best example of this biblical teaching is found in 1 Corinthians 2:14 (we will revisit the context of 1 Corinthians 1-3 many times in the pages ahead). This verse also has two parts to it; respectively, the emphasis of the first part falls on unregenerate man's hostility to the things of God, while the second probes more deeply into his depravity, focusing on his utter hopelessness. Both biblical estimations of fallen men are stated categorically: "But [i.e. in contrast with the Spirit-mediated gifts and abilities of vv. 6-13] a natural (or, an unspiritual) man [here *anthrōpos* has the generic connotation of *person*] does not accept (or, welcome [i.e. he is inhospitable to]) the things of the Spirit of God [ironically, by context, these are the 'Gospel things' which constitute his only hope], for they are foolishness [we get our word "moron" from this Greek term; so, we have returned to another biblical manifestation of man as the moral moron] to him, and he is not able to know them because they are spiritually examined" (i.e. investigated, appraised, evaluated, etc.; contextually, "discerned" [NIV]).

So the first clause of this verse reviews what the Bible says about humankind's perpetual resistance. However, it adds a statement about the 'reasoning' of the natural man in application to spiritual issues with eternal consequences. To his own self-destruction, he regards all spiritual things as nothing but silliness. Ironically, the "fool" (cf. Psalm 14:1; Romans 1:22; etc. again) looks upon the only remedy that can cure him, both spiritually and eternally, as "foolishness." He fights this help from Heaven with every ounce of his rebellious, autonomous being.

Furthermore, concerning the life-giving things of the Spirit, he has absolutely zero capacity to begin to understand or comprehend them [cf. the thrust of the negated verb for ability along with its complementary infinitive]. He is, both innately and deliberately, deaf and blind to spiritual things.

Preliminary Applications of It

In the light of man's original sin and total depravity which culminates in a hopeless state of inability, it should be becoming more obvious that his only hope is divine intervention. Natural man does not inherently possess the power to overcome his inability nor can merely finite rescue efforts give him sufficient impetus.

Let's look at it like this. Since fallen man is enslaved to self and to sin (cf., e.g. Romans 6:17-18, 20), his spiritual emancipation requires divine intervention and the resources of grace (see Part II forthcoming). More specifically, since his atheistic world-and-life view leaves him only in possession of an 'AM receiver' and since the Good News is broadcast on an 'FM (i.e. spiritual) band,' he needs to be divinely rewired and given a new antenna in order to receive and understand spiritual things. No mere methodologies of men can 'pull this off.' Trying *to do God's business man's way* 'won't cut it.'

For example, an evidentialist methodology accomplishes nothing except possibly to push natural man's arrogant deflections of the truth to a new, more sophisticated level of resistance. 'Everests' of evidences are incapable of converting him (note, e.g., the theological-methodological relevance of such passages as: Luke 16:27-31; John 2:23-25 [revisited]; 6:30 in the context of Jesus having just miraculously fed the five thousand; 9:13-16; 12:27-29; 12:39; etc.). The natural man's skewed thinking in the spiritual arena will reinterpret any 'logically' served-up, 'evidences' in an atheistic manner. He will resist all merely human 'reasonings' about spiritual things because his feet are set in the 'cement' of defiant rebellion.

Chapter 3

Remnants And Restrictions

So far, for the most part, I have been majoring on the universal ravages of total depravity for the unregenerate, including also the B. C. status of all believers. But what about the effects of depravity on a genuine disciple of our Lord Jesus Christ? Let me wander briefly between two biblical poles of reality.

On the one hand, the true child of God has been regenerated, but on the other hand, he has not yet been glorified. He's in process (i.e. sanctification). Although, he is not under the condemning reign of sin, he does periodically sin in thought, word, and deed. Furthermore, by God's great grace, he stands in union with Christ and the corporate body (i.e. the universal church). And yet, the Christian must put off the rags of the "old man" and progressively put on the holy garments of the "new man." Also, by the merciful interventions of the Lord, one who is positionally the "new man" also belongs to the inaugurated new age (genuine Christians are *biblical* 'new-agers'!). However, his eschatological 'already' progresses along an experiential 'not-yet' road to its ultimate divine destination. At times, he feels like he is living in a time warp.

These biblical tensions go on and on. However, the true disciple of Christ is no schizophrenic. Two 'people' do not coexist in him, one in a black hat, the other in a white one. Nevertheless, although his positional blessings in Christ are very real, so are evidences of his hamartiological [i.e. sinful] hangover. As a matter of fact, one of the earmarks of a maturing disciple is his recognition and revulsion of sin's remnants. True believers must not live in denial when it comes to their sin, nor will the Lord accept complacency with carnality. The latter attitude biblically would be characteristic of a pseudo disciple.

Intimations of Sin's Remnants

Appealing to several selected passages with minimal comment should document this particular doctrine. For example, one of the most mature disciples in the Old Testament was the author of the 119th Psalm. By God's grace and sufficient resources, namely the words from the Word, his maturity was obvious (cf., e.g., vv. 5, 11, 13-16, 22-24, 30-32, 47-48, 67, 93, 97-104, etc. [incidentally, some have accused him of braggadocio, but these and his other seemingly boastful testimonies are carefully couched in confirmations of dependence upon God]). Notwithstanding these evidences of significant maturity, he closes the psalm like this: "I have wandered about like a lost sheep; seek your servant, for I have not forgotten your words." As he grew in his comprehension of God's absolute holiness *and his own remnant sinfulness*, he ran from complacency and continued to plead for the gracious guidance of his LORD.

Concerning New Testament disciples, the picture is the same. Although hotly debated, I'm convinced that the exegetical evidence of Romans 7:14ff. supports the position that Paul is testifying herein of his *A. C.* life. As he more deeply ponders the purity of God's law and the terrorizing holiness of its Author, he sees his life not measuring up. This deeply disturbs him, however, not to the point of depression but rather to new levels of dependence. As in the case of initial salvation, so in the case of sanctification, Christ is our only hope. We are to keep on growing *in Him* (cf., e.g., 2 Peter 3:18).

Romans 12:1-2, Paul's ethical pivot-point in that great epistle, also supports the contention of remnant sin in the believer. As a matter of fact, there was a preview of these coming attractions back in chapter six. In Romans 6:1-11 the focus was upon God's gracious 'done' in Christ. Through solidarity with our Lord, we died with Him, were buried with Him, and were resurrected with Him.

However, for right now, if you will, He sends us back to earth "in order that . . . we also might walk [i.e. characteristically live our lives] in newness of life" (Romans 6:4b). As a vital constituent of this process, we need to reckon these solidarities with Christ as having great impact on our walk (cf. v. 11). Then comes the full application of these truths in vv. 12-13. Notice bound up in these exhortations, the real potential of sometimes living like a B. C. person: "Therefore, do not let sin reign as a king in your mortal body so as to keep on obeying its lusts, and do not (ongoingly) present your members [i.e. the parts of your body—in the Bible the "body" and its "members" are not the culpable agents but the instruments of the "you"; "bodies" and "members" do not commit sins, people do] as weapons of unrighteousness for sin, but rather present yourselves to God as being alive from the dead and your members as weapons of righteousness for God."

Now listen to the ethical echoes in Romans 12:1-2, paying special attention to the potentiality of sometimes living like a worldling. The corollary exhortations of v. 2 come from one two-edged sword: "I urgently implore you, brothers [i.e. professing Christian people], through the tender mercies of God to present your bodies a sacrifice, living, holy, well-pleasing to God, your logical (and/or, spiritual) service (or, worship). And do not be conformed to this age but be changed in form [cf. the English word "metamorphosis" which derives from this Greek word-group] by the renewal of the mind [this moral metamorphosis takes place on the battle ground of the mind – a 'change of mind,' i.e. repentance, is characteristic of salvation; renewal of mind is characteristic of sanctification], so that you might test (or, prove; or, approve; or, examine) what is the will (or, desire) of God, that which is good, and well pleasing (or acceptable), and perfect (or complete)." If sinning were not a real danger, the prohibitive part of his exhortation about sanctification would be a moot point.

Colossians 3 contains an important exhortation about: 1) not being who you were (i.e. B. C. people); 2) keeping on becoming who you are in Christ; and also 3) pressing on towards who you shall be in Him. According to biblical precedent, 'being' and thinking' interface in the first four verses of Colossians 3. Then in vv. 5-11, predicated upon union with Christ (cf. esp. vv. 1, 3), Paul urges his audience to apply their theological reckoning about these things (cf. v. 5a) to the practical 'stripping off' of representative unethical traits which characterize the "old man"(cf. vv. 8-9). Even in this section about divesting ourselves from the moral rags of the old man, a corresponding truth about the process of sanctification biblically resurfaces (i.e. the "new man" is in the process of being [likely a divine passive] renewed; cf. v. 10a). This latter thread of Paul's argument is taken up experientially with an emphasis on the believer's responsibility in vv. 12ff. We must continually keep getting dressed up in the wardrobe of righteousness. So, sanctification shows itself to be, once again, an interrelated, two-fold process of putting off sins and putting on holiness.

One of the clearest passages about intrusions of sin in the believer's life comes from John in his first epistle. He writes in 1 John 1:8, "If we should say [i.e. claim] that we do not have (or, do not possess) sin, (then) we deceive ourselves [i.e. we wander off course, or stray from reality] and the truth is not in us." Claiming that there is no sin principle in our life leads to self-deception and a denial of the truth. That is a dangerous position to be in. However, the exposing 'if . . . then' scenario of v. 10 is even more serious: "If we should say that we have not sinned [cf. '"we have not committed acts of sin'"] (then) we are making Him [i.e. God, vv. 5ff.] a liar and His word is not in us." Any denial of random acts of sin on the part of 'the claimer' is biblically unjustifiable. Furthermore, it would not compute with the merciful provision of v. 9 which confirms that the same blood that saves also sanctifies! Indeed, because of sins, His advocacy mercifully continues (2:1b).

So the presence of sins in the believer's life is undeniable. On the other hand, however, indications of patterns of sinfulness are absolutely unacceptable (cf. 1 John 2:1a plus the many, ethical yardsticks that John gives to measure genuine spiritual life).

Implications of Sin's Restrictions

Although the believer has a new world-and-life view, one which is theocentric in orientation, he still periodically suffers from resurgences of man-centeredness. He sometimes exhibits indications of a man-centered hangover. Instead of operating consistently dependently, autonomous pride raises its ugly head. The significance of this phenomenon in application to ministry should never be underestimated. If you happen to be a pastor or one who serves in another area of full-time Christian service, the reality of 'pride in the pew' does not come as a surprise to you. But, I want to bring this truth even closer to home. There is far too much 'pride behind the pulpit'.

Concerning believers who have been regenerated and whose basic world-and-life view has been turned right side up by the grace of our Lord, they still exhibit episodes of resistance. Although they have been given an FM receiver and antenna, now and again their reception is poor. Sin short circuits their equipment, and sometimes pride even bends their antennas away from spiritual truths or Christian evidences. (Christian evidences are basically for Christians; they are like condiments sprinkled on *inscripturated* truths for believers.) For example, do you remember what happened in Mark, chapter six after Jesus had miraculously fed the five thousand and sent His disciples on ahead by boat? As they were exerting themselves rowing into a strong head wind, Jesus came walking on the sea. First, they were frightened because they thought that He was a ghost (v. 5a). Then Mark notes 1) that He spoke to them; 2) He got into the boat; and then 3) immediately there was a dead calm (Mark 6:50b-51a). Now catch this about this inner core of His disciples (i.e. the apostles no less), "they were completely amazed, for they had not understood about the loaves; their hearts were hardened" (Mark 6:51b-52, NIV). They experienced a mental malfunction (they still had not spiritually put the pieces together about the stupendous miracle that they had witnessed hours earlier). Why? Because "their heart was hardened" (i.e. their core of being was callused and therefore impervious to the evidence). An isolated occasion? Not hardly.

How about Luke 24? From six months, up to as long as a year before His passion week, our Lord was teaching His own about the events that would transpire in Jerusalem (cf., e.g., Matthew 16:21). And yet, after the women who had gone to the tomb to anoint Christ's body were convinced by angelic testimony that He had been raised just as He had predicted, and after they had run back to tell the apostles the great news, how did the elite inner circle respond? Well, Dr. Luke says that the apostles diagnosed the women as being 'delirious' [the medical background of the term normally rendered as "nonsense" in v. 11]. And furthermore, he reports that they *refused* to believe them (i.e. "they would not believe" is expressed as a persisting resistance). If those kinds of responses of resistance were exhibited on occasion by Christ's chosen leaders for His infant church, should we expect anything different from all the sheep of His flock? To say the least, Christians are not very reasonable at times, and it takes a lot more than skillful rhetoric and logic to get their thinking and behaving back on track.

Tragically the most culpable manifestation of persisting pride in the believer occurs when someone who claims *to be doing God's business* tries to carry out his responsibilities *man's way*. Also, unfortunately, speaking as a former seminary professor for more than twenty years, I have seen the most serious offenses come from the ranks of the most credentialed people. The 'professional' pastor, theologian, apologist, etc., is most vulnerable. Attitudes of arrogance will prohibit us from *doing God's business His way.*

Hear an important testimony from the apostle Paul! He personally knew the devastating potential of the hazard of pride in the person 'behind the pulpit' (cf., e.g., 2 Corinthians 12:7). Although his credentials were exceedingly noteworthy by the standards of man (cf., e.g., Acts 22:3; Philippians 3:4-6; etc.), he refused *to do God's business man's way.* We will see *why* later in Part III when 1 Corinthians 2:1-5 is discussed in detail. But for right now, as a warning light to each and everyone of us, lay witness and full-time Christian servant alike, I want to connect Philippians 3:3b-4 with Paul's controlling ministerial attitude expressed in condensed form in 2 Corinthians 10:3-5. "We [i.e. true believers] . . . put no confidence in the flesh, although I myself might have confidence even in the flesh. If anyone else has a mind to put confidence in the flesh, I far more" (Philippians 3:3b-4, NASB). . . . "For even though we are walking in flesh [i.e. living in a condition of creaturely weakness, in possession of only finite resources], we are not warring according to the flesh [i.e. we are not conducting our Christian campaigns in accordance with and as measured by finite and fallen resources], for the weapons of our warfare are not fleshly (weapons) but rather are powerful (weapons) in connection with God, (suitable) for the destruction of fortresses [cf. the sufficiencies of God discussed in Part II], [consequently with these weapons] we are destroying arguments (or, speculations; or, sophistries; etc.) and every arrogant thing that rises up against (or, resists) the knowledge of God and we are taking every thought captive [i.e. making it a P. O. W.] unto the obedience of Christ" [i.e. making it obedient to Christ]. Pride in ministry must be avoided like the plague since it cuts us off from the true power of God. Ministering according to the flesh (i.e. autonomously and independently) is a contradiction of Christianity. The prideful 'knee' of the heart must bow to God and His ways of doing things. Christ's disciples were dependent in the reception of their salvation, and they must remain dependent throughout the process of their sanctification, including also how they carry on *God's business*

Chapter 4
Satanic Complications

By now, some of you may be saying, "It's hard to imagine how things could get any worse than this." Sorry, they can. Besides the hopelessness of natural men being utterly dominated by sin and believers still being vulnerable to sins, the archenemy of God and of humankind, Satan, is carrying on his wicked warfare like a roaring and roaming lion (1 Peter 5:8). However, he usually carries on his campaigns very subtlety, since he is a slick and slippery schemer.

In the area of Satanology (i.e. the study of Satan), there is special need for biblical balance. We must not give him more than his due (what I have called a Flip Wilson "the-devil-made-me-do-it" theology, i.e. one that passes 'every buck' of failure on to him). Nevertheless, we must pay attention to what the Bible ascribes to him, that is, superhuman strength (so much so, that even Michael, the archangel, would not engage him apart from divine authority [Jude 9] – What does this say about so-called 'deliverance ministries,' etc.?). Until his millennial incarceration revealed in Revelation 20:1-3 and his ultimate, eternal consignment to the lake of fire (cf., e.g., Matthew 25:41 and Revelation 20:10), he remains on the rampage, specializing both in the blinding of the blind and the accusing of the brothers (i.e. fellow-Christians). Because of this, it seems best to consider these two targeted constituencies in this order.

His Tatics with the Lost

Being their "father" (e.g. John 8:44), he has sort of a symbiotic relationship with the unsaved. For example, they seem to be snuggled down comfortably in his lap (cf., e.g., 1 John 5:19b). He has a vested interest in keeping them from Christ by "(effectually) operating among the sons of disobedience" (Ephesians 2:2b). Therefore, concerning the lost, he is committed to making them all the more blind to the liberating things of Christ. This truth should have an impact on our evangelistic methods. If this superhuman evil being engages himself in veiling the Gospel from unbelievers by powerfully blinding their minds (2 Corinthians 4:3-4), how can we, by using puny weapons of the flesh, have a chance at rescuing them? We can't apart from God and the 'nuclear' weapons our Lord has made available to us (cf. Part II).

His Tactics Against the Saved

Besides causing significant troubles in the evangelistic theater of the battle, the archenemy also engages himself on another front, our efforts towards edification. Paul put it this way when writing to professing Christians at Corinth: "But I am fearful lest some how, as the serpent deceived [i.e. spiritually seduced] Eve by his cunning, your minds should be corrupted from sincerity and purity in regard to Christ." Paul was exceedingly concerned about the vulnerability of the Corinthians in the face of the skillful schemes of Satan. Not coincidentally nor without significance, did you notice that his special target is mankind's *mind*, whether the sin and self-enslaved mind of unbelievers (2 Corinthians 4:4) or the susceptible-to-sin minds of professing believers here in 2 Corinthians 11:3? The noetic complications of the race are catalyzed all the more by the devil.

Anyone claiming to *do God's business,* must be fully aware of the devil's *designs* (2 Corinthians 2:11) and *devices* (cf. Ephesians 6:11; cf. also, Ephesians 4:14; this particular word for "schemes," or "stratagems" comes over into English from Greek as '*methodologies*'). Besides possessing a biblical awareness about him, we need to put on God's armor in order to withstand him (Ephesians 6:10ff.). The military imagery of this passage is ear-and eye-catching.

Verses 10-17 emphasize the full armor of God which Christians must take up and put on. Nearly all of these accouterments are defensive in nature, except the "sword" of verse 17b. Furthermore, you can put a uniform on a man but that doesn't make him a soldier. He needs the demeanor and the 'military bearing' of a loyal member of the ranks. In this case, a Christian's 'bearing' is prayer, the primary indicator of *dependence* on God who is our Commander-in-Chief.

Loyalty is tested by following orders, and these orders are clear: "be strong!" (v. 10) [i.e. a divine passive; 'keep on being in-strengthened by the Person and provisions of the Lord']; "enclothe yourselves with the full armor of God in order to/so that you might be able to stand . . . !" (v. 11); "take up . . . that you might be able to withstand (or, resist)!" (v. 13 [cf. also James 4:6b; 1 Peter 5:9]); "therefore stand!" (v. 14); "in all, taking up [the participle carries the imperatival weight of the context] the shield of faith by means of which you will be able to extinguish the fiery projectiles of the evil one!" (v. 16); and "receive the helmet of salvation" (v. 17). These repetitions reinforce the nature of our warfare as dictated by our commanding General. He does not say search for and charge the diabolical enemy like people of the 'spiritual warfare' movement urge. Why? Well, one important reason is found in v. 12. We are not fighting against mere men but against henchmen from hell with superhuman strategies and weaponries. Any overconfidence on our part in our own personal bravery is a quick formula for defeat. We must look to the One who alone is stronger (God is omnipotent!) than the ancient enemy and his armies. These truths constitute another reason why Paul testified as he did in 2 Corinthians 10:3-5. Conventional carnal weapons will always prove themselves to be inadequate; we need to rely dependently upon God's nuclear capabilities (again, cf. Part II, Chapter 6, forthcoming).

Part II
Salvation And Sufficiencies

Chapter 5
The Sovereignty of God In Salvation

Remember that a superficial diagnosis of the depravity of man will lead to insufficient rem-edies for his cure. The biblical diagnosis is that the race is spiritually dead because of their innate heart trouble (cf., e.g., Ephesians 2:1-3, again). In and of themselves, they are helpless and hopeless. Their only hope lies outside of themselves in God. Here is where the merciful "BUT GOD" comes in to cure (cf., e.g., Ephesians 2:4ff). Without denying that a biblically defined human responsibility is involved in both delivering the cure and receiving the cure (cf., e.g., Romans 10:13-15), salvation is pre-eminently God's business. The theological bottom-line of the regeneration of any individual is the sovereign grace of our Lord.

Sample Assertions of This Fact

Although the Old Testament usually speaks of salvation in terms of a temporal deliverance or rescue from some crisis (e.g., cf. most of the "save me" prayers from the Psalms), on occasion the context of the divine deliverance spiritually and eternally transcends any mere rescue from an attacking army, etc. Indeed, sometimes one runs into a non-restricted, all-inclusive reference to God's salvation. Such is the case in the proverbial proclamation of Psalm 3:8a: "Salvation belongs to the LORD." There are only two words in the Hebrew text here, one from the most common and frequently occurring word-group for "salvation" in the Old Testament (i.e. *yasha*) and the other God's name "Yahweh" with a possessive use of a proposition attached to it. Consequently, the implication of this exclamation is that the LORD uniquely owns and soverignly bestows deliverance of all kinds.

Turning to the New Testament for pattern passages, Titus 3:5 presents itself as an excellent representative of the sovereignty of God in salvation. Titus 3:3-7 unfolds just like Ephesians 2:1-10. Verse 3 of Titus 3 summarizes our helpless and hopeless estate in sin (i.e. our B. C. condition), then v. 4 crashes through with an attestation of the inexplicable, inscrutable grace of God (cf. Ephesians 2:4). As in the case of Ephesians 2:5-6, Titus 3:5-7 is a synopsis of what God has wondrously done for us. Although verses 4-7 of Titus 3 constitute one complex sentence in the Greek text, its main framework is found at the outset of v. 5, i.e. "He [i.e. God, v.4] saved us"! And just to make sure we understand upon what grounds He eternally rescued us, the Spirit through Paul's pen adds, "not out of (i.e. because of) works which we did in righteousness [i.e. this would have been impossible; cf., e.g., Isaiah 64:6], but rather according to (i.e. based on) His mercy. . . ." Our spiritual bankruptcy leads only to death, not life. If there is to be true spiritual life (i.e. eternal life), it is due to God mercifully taking the initiative in regeneration and renewal (v. 5b).

Sample Amplifications of This Fact

God is the Architect of Salvation

Here and there the Bible allows us to peek behind the curtain of the creation, the Fall, and God's merciful act of saving of some people from eternal condemnation. Before He laid the foundations of the universe, the Triune God drew up a master plan which included the selection and salvation of certain recipients of His special grace. This plan was not skeletal nor vague but comprehensive and specific. It included not just the choice of the recipients of salvation but also the provisions and applications necessary to realize deliverances in time, space, and history.

Central to these divine provisions was the death of Christ. For example, a viably alternate punctuation of

Revelation 13:8b speaks of "the book of life belonging to the Lamb [i.e. Christ] that was slain from the creation of the world" (NIV). That overwhelming truth is expanded upon in the poetic prophecy of Isaiah 53. Two major themes run through Isaiah 40-66, God is sovereign and God is redeemer. They both converge in this 53rd chapter. These verses outline God's plan and providence for the historical actualization of His eternal blueprint for salvation through Messiah. Verses 4ff. focus on our sin and the Father's substitutionary sacrifice of His Son. The passives at the beginning of v. 5, i.e. "He was pierced" and "He was crushed," are divine passives as clearly documented by the overt affirmations of vv. 6b and 10a, i.e. "but the LORD [i.e. inspite of our own defiant waywardness] has caused the iniquity of all of us to strike against Him"; "But the LORD [i.e. although the suffering Servant was absolutely sinless, v. 9b] was pleased [cf. the NIV: "it was the LORD's will"] to crush Him. . . ." So this amazing 'Fourth Servant Song' is a vital prophetic link in a chain of grace anchored in eternity past, fulfilled in Christ and His cross, and extending into eternity future as to the fruits of the Suffering Servant's loving obedience (cf., e.g., v. 11b).

Another important passage which peeks behind the scenes and captures glimpses of the divine decree as applied to the salvation of sinners is Ephesians 1:3-14. One very long, complex sentence in the original, this text is exclusively God-centered. As in the case of Isaiah 53, the be-graced beneficiaries of this marvelous plan have nothing to boast about except God (cf. the axiomatic truth of Jeremiah 9:23-24). No wonder a doxology launches this passage (Ephesians 1:3) and three climatic outbursts of thanksgiving punctuate its transcendent teachings about the sovereignty of God in salvation (cf. vv. 6, 12, 14). Although all the persons of the Godhead are noted to be actively involved in the implementation of the plan (cf. the focus on the Son in vv. 7-13a and on a particular ministry of the Spirit in vv. 13b-14), the grammar of the passage puts a special emphasis on the Father as the originator of this eternally significant decree. It is He who "chose (or, elected) us in Him [i.e. in Christ; cf. the "in Christ" at the end of v. 3] before the foundation of the world" (v. 4). This statement constitutes the structural and theological backbone of the whole passage. Then some of the attendant blessings flowing out from our election in eternity past are surveyed: 1) predestination to adoption (vv. 5-6), 2) redemption (vv. 7-8a), 3) enlightenment (vv. 8b-10), 4) inheritance (vv. 11-12), and 5) divine sealing (vv. 13-14).

These great messages about the sovereign grace of God in salvation are compressed even more tightly into such theological packages as 2 Timothy 1:8-10:

> So do not be ashamed to testify about our Lord, or ashamed of me [i.e. Paul] his prisoner. But join with me in suffering for the gospel, by the power of God, who has saved us [i.e. only God's power can rescue us] and called us to a holy life—not because of anything we have done [i.e. we couldn't have done anything to rescue ourselves; we are bankrupt of spiritual resources and power] but because of His own purpose and grace [i.e. the bottom-line always comes out to be His inexplicable sovereign grace]. This grace was given us in Christ Jesus before the beginning of time, but it has now been revealed through the appearing of our Savior, Christ Jesus, who has destroyed death and has brought life and immortality to light through the gospel (NIV).

God the Father is indeed the sovereign architect of a spiritual blueprint drawn up in eternity past which includes the provision, means, and application of salvation.

God Takes the Initiative in Salvation

Since fallen man will not nor cannot seek God, when any person is saved guess who always takes the initiative? Furthermore, because of remnants of resistance among the saved, He also is biblically recognized as taking the initiative among them. Once again, such scriptural teachings must not be fabricated into a theological system which denies human responsibility. Real responsibility is there also according to biblical declarations and documentations; however, the issue is one of balance, of keeping the theological cart (i.e. the responsibilities of men) behind the horse (i.e. the initiative of God). A few biblical scenarios should suffice.

Jeremiah in Lamentations 5:21a (cf. Jeremiah 31:18-19) passionately appeals to God: "Turn us, O LORD, to yourself, then we shall turn (or, return)." Jeremiah was painfully acquainted with the resistance of Judah and God's just judgment upon the people. That is why, using a bold command built upon the primary word-group for "repentance" in the Old Testament, the prophet implores the LORD to cause an about-face of the people to God. In essence he prays, "Cause us to repent, that we may repent." If there was going to be a revival among the professing people of God, the God of the people needed to take the initiative and empower them to return.

Listen to a couple of short, corroborative passages out of Matthew. Christ speaking about the only way sinful men will receive the spiritual truths that lead to salvation says,

> I praise Thee, O Father, Lord of heaven and earth, that Thou didst hide these things from the wise and intelligent [i.e. an ironic statement; these are the mental morons who resist the things of the Spirit] and reveal them to babes [the infant imagery emphasizes dependence]. Yes, Father, for thus it was well-pleas-

ing in Thy sight. All things have been handed over to Me by my Father [cf. His bestowed authority in the Great Commission; Matthew 28:18]; and no one knows [i.e. no person has accessibility to real spiritual knowledge, in and of himself] the Son [i.e. He who is the Savior], except the Father; nor does anyone know the Father, except the Son, and anyone to whom the Son wills to reveal Him (Matthew 11:25-27, NASB).

Apart from Christ's sovereign will to unveil the truths of divine deliverance to men with blinded eyes and deaf ears there would be absolutely no hope. But He has revealed Himself and the Father to those chosen from before the foundation of the world. By the way, this fact of special knowledge specially conveyed to certain ones, does not deny that they must approach the Revealer-Savior (cf. vv. 28-30).

In Matthew 16:15-17 we find the account of Christ's evaluation of Peter's 'good confession' (just preceding the record of that impetuous apostle's 'bad confession'!). After quizzing the disciples on who the people were saying that Jesus was (vv. 13-14), our Lord put this question directly to His special core of disciples (v. 15), and Peter, the quick-responding spokesman of the group, answered, "You are the Messiah, the Son of the living God" (v. 16). It is significant that Christ did not say, 'Good for you, Peter, you have come to the proper conclusion by using your reasoning and by weighing all the evidences you have witnessed.' Rather our Lord says, " 'Blessed are you, Simon son of Jonah, for this was not revealed to you by man [i.e. literally, "flesh and blood," an idiomatic combination for humankind as being finite, frail, and fallen], but by my Father in heaven'" (v. 17, NIV). This kind of divine initiative and intervention is necessary when rescuing people who both resist and do not have the capacity to understand and appropriate the spiritual things which are prerequisites for salvation (cf. 1 Corinthians 2:14, again).

Now is a good time to revisit Romans 5:6-11. Remember how our B. C. state was described therein; we were without spiritual strength (v. 6); we were failures morally (v. 8); and we were active enemies of God (v. 10). Even though or while we were still in those conditions, Christ died for us (vv. 6, 8) and we were reconciled to God through His crosswork (v. 10). These scenarios again show salvation to be God-centered; He takes the initiative with people who won't and can't.

While we're in Romans, let's go to chapter 9. In Romans 9:16 we find a condensed theological affirmation that biblically qualifies as a doctrinal maxim. In a context which magnifies the mercy of the Lord, Paul concludes very literally, "Consequently then, it [i.e. the "it" is left deliberately unidentified, contributing to the aphoristic nature of this assertion] is not of the one [i.e. from the source of a human being] who desires (or, "who is willing"; cf. and contrast God's 'willing' in vv. 18 and 22), neither of the one who runs, but of the merciful God." The NIV's dynamic rendering is smooth and it captures the thrust of Paul's point: "It does not, therefore, depend on man's desire or effort, but on God's mercy." It must be restated at this juncture that Paul is not prohibiting all willing and running, but only those autonomous efforts that seek to inflate the 'abilities' of humanity and thereby impugn the prerogatives of a sovereign God.

As intimated earlier, God also takes the initiative throughout the sanctification process of believers. For example, in Paul's introductory thanksgiving to God for the Philippian converts (Philippians 1:3ff), He joyfully confesses his confidence in the Lord that He would sustain and complete His work of salvation among the people. The apostle was fond of the Philippians and commended them in many ways, but his confidence that they would ultimately persevere and reach the goal of glorification was not grounded on them and mere human effort. Verse

6 reads like this: "being confident (i.e. I am standing persuaded) of this very thing, that one who has begun [i.e. God had commenced *His* work, v. 3] a good work in you will bring it to completion until the day of Christ Jesus." So, because of God, genuine believers will get from 'here' to 'there.' The continuing process of getting from 'here' to 'there' is taken up in such passages as 2 Corinthians 3:18; 4:16; Colossians 3:10; etc. For example, in 2 Corinthians 4:16 the on-going hand of God in salvation is highlighted with the words "our inner man is being renewed [a divine passive; God is the agent of this renewal] day by day."

The testimony of Philippians 2:12-13 is strategic in that it places the sovereignty of God right beside the responsibility of believers in the sanctification process. Verse 12 must not be considered without the truth of verse 13, and vice versa. Right after Paul's ethical exhortations that the church live single-mindedly and selflessly based upon the ultimate attitudinal example of Christ (i.e. 1:27-2:11), he urges the Philippians to action with these words:

> Therefore, my beloved ones, just as always you have obeyed, not only in my presence but now much more in my absence, with fear and trembling [remember that the fear of God is "*the beginning*" of all true knowledge and the practical wisdom for life's pathways (cf., e.g., Psalm 111:10; Proverbs 1:7; 9:10; Matthew 10:28; Hebrews 10:31; etc.); a healthy fear of our holy and righteous God is intended to be a primary motivation for holy living], keep on working out your own salvation [i.e. progressive *sanctification*], for God is the One who is (effectually) working among you both to will [i.e. on-goingly throughout the process] and to perform (or, do; i.e. to keep on achieving) for the sake of His good pleasure (Philippians 2:12-13).

Although believers are to apply themselves responsibly throughout sanctification process, they need to understand that their gracious Lord is the continuous Energizer of both their volition and their performance. God not only initiates salvation in His objects of grace, but He also consistently provides the dynamic for their sanctification.

Just prior to pushing onward to some illustrations of the sovereignty of God in salvation, I would like to offer Romans 8:28-30 as a panoramic review of the ground we've just covered. Verse 28 provides the bird's-eye view: "Now we know that all things [accepting the reading that "all things" is the subject of this clause; God nevertheless is the *implied* subject who sovereignly directs these things to their appointed ends from behind the scenes] are working together unto good [i.e. God's good goal] in reference to the ones who love God, in reference to those who are called ones according to His purpose." This is a very important foundation stone for Paul's whole argument on the security of the true disciples in chapter 8 (note this chapter begins with "no condemnation" in v. 1 and ends with 'no separation' in vv. 35-39).

To document the sweeping affirmations of v. 28, vv. 29-30 point to the awesome deeds of God in salvation. These five divine deeds are selected links of salvation which form an unbroken chain of grace which is anchored in eternity past, moves on into our time, space, and history zone, and reaches to eternity future. Each one of them is stated as a 'done deal': "For whom God foreknew [i.e. intimately loved beforehand in an elective sense; cf., e.g., the combined theological impact of 'knowing' in Genesis 18:19, Exodus 2:25; Psalms 1:6; 144:3; Jeremiah 1:5; Hosea 13:5; Amos 3:2; Matthew 7:23; John 10:14-15; Acts 2:23; 1 Corinthians 8:3; Galatians 4:9; 2 Timothy 2:19; and 1 John 3:1], He also predestined [i.e. marked out ahead of time, predetermined] to be conformed to the image of His Son so that He might be first-born among many brothers; and whom He predestined, these also He called [i.e. effectually], and these also He justified [i.e. He declared them to be righteous in Christ]; and whom He justified these also He glorified." The only comments that seem appropriate from the beneficiaries of such sovereign grace are a praiseful "Wow!" and "Thank you, Lord!"

Sample Illustrations of This Fact

God's sovereignty in salvation, from start to finish, is wonderously illustrated throughout the Scriptures. A few historical affirmations and testimonies will bear this out.

Deuteronomy 7:6-11 speaks of the LORD's sovereign choice of Israel as His special nation. This people of God was ordered to do some seemingly horrific things to other peoples in the first five verses of this chapter [cf., e.g., the command 'to totally wipe them out,' in v. 2, a command *not* based upon the fact that Israel was innately better than the other nations, but based upon the unflinching holiness of Israel's electing God]. The transcendent reasoning behind those seemingly harsh demands begins with the explanatory "for" which launches v. 6. Moses writes: "For (or, because; or, since) you are a holy (or, sanctified; or, set apart) people to the LORD your God, the LORD your God chose (or, elected) you to be, in reference to Himself, a specially treasured people out from among all the peoples that are upon the face of the ground [i.e. from all the peoples on earth]. The LORD did not set His special love upon you or choose you because you were greater (or, more numerous) than all the peoples, for you were the least (or, fewest) of all the peoples, but because the LORD loved you and kept the oath which He had sworn to your fathers; . . ." (Deuteronomy 7:6-8a). These verses describe the fact of and reason for Israel's election. However, when it gets down to expressing that reason it seems like double-talk, that is, 'God specially loved and elected you . . . because He loved you!' (vv. 6, 8). This is complicated even further by the absolute denial of any merit or mass (i.e. numbers) to this insignificant nation of the Ancient Near East (v. 7). The reason why this reason for God's election of Israel seems like double-talk is because it is an accurate portrayal of His sovereign grace in operation. The unique grace of God as spelled out in the Bible is essentially inscrutable. In modern lingo it blows our minds, especially the minds of the unworthy recipients of divine mercy.

Before we journey on, please permit me to comment briefly on the application of the benefits of sovereign grace to holy living. This passage from Deuteronomy 7 is not merely theologically informative, it is ethically demanding. The great 'dones' of God in vv. 6-10 are designed to stimulate an ethical responsibility in the people 'to do' (cf. v. 11). However, in rightly stressing human responsibility, we should not assume that Israel would have been left to her own inadequate resources (cf. the sustained grace of God in providing the necessary sufficiencies for sanctification, e.g., in the prayer of Solomon in 1 Kings 8:57-58).

Moving from the corporate nation Israel to a selected Old Testament saint, listen to the personal testimony of the author of Psalm 119. In v. 93, he attests: "I will never forget Your precepts, because by means of them [cf. the emphasis on the Word of God in Chapter 6 coming shortly] You [i.e. Yahweh-God] gave me life." The leading causative verb is often translated You "revived me" (NASB) or "You have renewed my life" (NIV). In most Old Testament contexts, revival is the connotation; however, here, in this setting, the emphasis seems to be on the fact that the LORD had graciously imparted initial life to him (i.e. not just temporal life, but spiritual life with its potentialities of abundant blessing; cf., e.g., life, i.e. living [same root], in Deuteronomy 8:3).

Now let's spend some time in the Book of Acts, a rich repository of historical examples. In Acts 9:32-11:18 we

find Luke's account of the events leading up to and stemming from the conversion of Cornelius and company. All
these events resounded the sovereign grace and providence of God in salvation (cf., e.g., Cornelius' vision in
10:1-8; Peter's vision in 10:9-16; Peter and Cornelius
'comparing notes' on God's providential preparations in
10:28-33; Peter's preaching in 10:34-43; God's making the
words of the Gospel effectual in 10:44-48; and Peter's testimony to the initially skeptical 'kosher' majority back in
Jerusalem in 11:4-17). The punch-line of Acts 11:18, however, summarizes the theological thrust of the whole story. Once the 'elitist' Jewish Christians realized that they
were not so elite anymore, they praised God for what He
had obviously brought to pass. Luke puts it this way,
"Now when they heard these things, they became quiet
and glorified God, saying, 'So then, even to the Gentiles,
God has given the repentance unto life.'" God is clearly
noted to be the author and activator of salvation; He
grants the radical '180' (i.e. repentance; 'change of mind')
that is prerequisite for spiritual life.

After Paul and Barnabas had completed their first
missionary journey, they returned to Antioch to give a report to their sending church. The gist of all that had tran-
spired on that circuit is capsulized in Acts 14:27: "And
when they had arrived and gathered the church together,
they *began* to report all things that God had done with
them [possibly, with the sense "through them" (NIV)]
and how He had opened a door of faith to the Gentiles"
(NASB). They fully recognized that eternal results are
brought to pass only by divine intervention. Speaking of
God 'opening doors,' remember what He had done in Lydia's heart during Paul's second missionary journey. To
be sure, as usual, Paul was preaching his heart out (cf.,
e.g. Acts 16:10b with v. 13b), and also on this occasion this
lady was listening to the words of the Gospel (v. 14a), but
it was the LORD who powerfully effectuated the spiritual results. The NIV reads, "The Lord opened her heart to

respond to Paul's message" (v. 14b). More periphrastically and interpretively, "The Lord, who is the sovereign Savior, He who diagnoses the terminal condition of the human heart, He who is the exclusive "heart-knower" (e.g. Acts 1:24; 15:8) and "heart transplanter" (e.g. Ezekiel 11:19), graciously opened the sin-shut doors of Lydia's heart to turn her mind to, i.e. to pay attention to and respond to, the things of the Gospel which were being spoken by Paul."

One of several personal testimonies about the Apostle Paul's conversion and commission is found in Acts 26. As he stood before Agrippa and recounted his Damascus Road experience, a long, complex sentence stands out as a significant monument to the sovereignty of God in Paul's salvation. The Lord's commands (v. 16a), His sovereign and purposeful appointment of Paul (v. 16b), His revelations to the apostle (v. 16c), His promised protection of him (v. 17) and His ultimate purpose for his ministry (v. 18) all combine to verify that salvation is pre-eminently God's business. Paul understood this basic truth from the beginning, and it never grew dim as he labored till death for Christ.

The essentials of Paul's commission as sketched out in Acts 26, were illustrated applicationally throughout his missionary 'career.' Take for example, what he says about the disciples in Thessalonica. These are his words of testimony and praise found in 2 Thessalonians 2:13-14: "But we [an emphatic "we"] ought [an 'I. O. U.' term] to keep on giving thanks to God at all times concerning you [i.e. the conversion of the believers at Thessalonica provided the occasion for Paul's praise to God], brothers beloved by the Lord, because God chose you from the beginning [a viable variant reads "(as) firstfruits"] for salvation [i.e. unto the goal of salvation; cf. the NIV's dynamic "to be saved"] by the sanctification of the Spirit and by faith in the truth, unto which also He called you through our Gospel unto the goal of obtaining glory, that of our Lord

Jesus Christ." These verses, although highly concentrated, seem to cover all the bases of God's sovereignty in
salvation. From the perspective of theology proper, all
three Persons of the Trinity are seen as being involved in
salvation, God the Father in v. 13a, the Spirit in 13b, and
the Son in v. 14b. Timewise, the events move from an
election to salvation in eternity past to regeneration, then
through sanctification to glorification in the future (v. 13).
As to God's sovereignty working through means, both
faith in the Gospel (v. 13b) and the preaching of the Gospel (v. 14a) are mentioned. However, as the leading verbs
indicate it is God who engineers and energizes the whole
process. No wonder all thanksgiving goes to Him.

Sample Implications of this Fact

Such representative texts as those above carry along
with them much methodological freight. Minimally, they
show the centrality of God in salvation, and hopefully,
that inescapable scriptural truth should help hold back
the reigns of unbridled human tactics in ministry. To
tighten those reigns a little more, I would like to offer
two more passages for your consideration.

The first sample text could be classified as THEO-
LOGICAL-methodological. It comes from the lips of our
Lord in John, chapter 6. Actually, He gives three varia-
tions on the same Biblical truth. In v. 37, he expresses this
truth generally and positively, affirming: "All that [the
neuter construction indicates that He is stating what follows as an axiomatic truth] the Father gives to me [cf. the
structure and theology of John 17:2: "all that has been
given to Him (i.e. to the Son by the Father), to them (now
individualized and personalized) He should give to them
(i.e. the elect) life eternal"] will come unto Me, and the
one who comes unto Me I will never ever [bad English,
good Greek] cast out." Now dogmatically and negatively
He says in v. 44a: "No one can come to Me [i.e. not one
person has the ability to come to Christ] unless (or, ex-

cept) the Father who has sent Me should draw him" [i.e. effectually call and successfully bring him to Christ]. Finally Christ *negatively applies* this dogmatic dictum about divine drawing to many who were standing there and chafing at His words: "'But there are some of you who do not believe.' For Jesus know from the beginning who they were who did not believe, and who it was that would betray Him. And He was saying, 'For this reason I have said to you, that no one can come to Me, unless, it has been granted him from the Father'" (vv. 64-65, NASB).

Now listen to Paul's theological-METHODOLOGICAL testimony in 1 Corinthians 3:5-7: "What, after all, is Apollos? And what is Paul? Only servants, through whom you come to believe—as the Lord assigned to each his task. I planted the seed, Apollos watered it, but God made it grow. So neither he who plants nor he who waters is anything, but only God, who makes things grow" (NIV). As Paul talks about himself and Apollos, he doesn't even say "Who?" but says "What?" Herein, this language is more than proverbial; it is also polemical. He is still dealing with the factions among the Corinthians, in this case, their preferences for different preachers (cf., e.g., 1 Corinthians 1:12-13). He is not demeaning Apollos' labors nor his own. After all, they were the channels "through whom" the Corinthians had come to profess faith in Christ. However, he was determined to put things into their divine context with his "BUT GOD" statements of fact (cf. again vv. 6b and 7b). So, since salvation is essentially God's business, we, like Paul, need to commit ourselves to *doing that business His way.*

Chapter 6
The Sufficiencies
Of God For Service

Since the natural man is a child of the devil, sold out to self and sin, and since we in our own resources are impotent 'medics,' some of you might be thinking, "Then how can *we* ever share spiritual things with the lost?" Furthermore, since all believers, although positionally having had their deep tap root of sin graciously cut by God, experientially still have some feeder roots reaching out into the soil of sin, "How could we possibly minister to the body of Christ so as to exhort and edify one another?" Without denying that we really are hopeless and helpless in these hands-on areas by the standard of our innate finiteness and remnant fallenness, we children of God are not left to share and to serve without efficient provisions from our heavenly Father.

He has indeed abundantly provided divine resources for us to do *His business His way.* These are *His* special weapons for *true* spiritual warfare. Our tangible weapon in hand (i.e. Our Sufficiency in Hand) is the Word of God, and our intangible weapon (i.e. Our Sufficiency 'in Heart') is the Person of the Spirit of God Himself. Spiritually considered, these divine nuclear weapons are not optional but absolutely necessary for ministry. The effectual dynamic of the Spirit of God working with the Word of God alone can save and sanctify sinners.

Our Sufficiency in Hand

Our more tangible divine sufficiency should always be in our hands and/or "treasured up" in our hearts. It is our propositional weapon. This Word of God is powerfully dynamic and absolutely sufficient on all fronts of the spiritual battlefield. Some sample references will exegetically confirm its nuclear capabilities.

Let's begin in the Psalms. Psalm 19 is familiar territory. Most Christians recognize that it divides logically into two parts: 1) the revelation of God in nature (i.e. vv. 1-6; we've already noted in Romans 1:18ff. that this general revelation is insufficient for salvation, because of man's sinful resistance; it condemns rather than converts), and 2) the revelation of God in Scripture (i.e. vv. 7-14; this special revelation, as we're going to see, proves itself to be sufficient both for salvation and for sanctification). In verses 7ff. the psalmist employs five words for the Word, five synonyms for Scripture in its totality (cf. eight of them in Psalm 119). Later he mentions the personal affect of the Word of God in believers, that is, "fear" in v. 9a. In the last part of the psalm he personally praises God for His Word and prays for the integrity of life that is revealed by the Scriptures. But I want to focus on the axiomatic truths about Scripture in vv. 7-8. Each of these four poetic lines contains an affirmation about what the Word of God is and an attestation to what it effectually *does*. Furthermore, each of the four attestions about what it dynamically accomplishes is conveyed by a causative and characterizing participle.

The first line (i.e. v. 7a) says, "The Law of the LORD is sound [this Hebrew word, translated as "blameless" in the early Greek translation of the Old Testament (the LXX), is more positive in its description; the word-group in Hebrew has a common denominator of 'having integrity'; cf. the translation "perfect" in the NASV, NIV, etc.], causing the soul to turn around." First, it is necessary to explain the term "Law" in contexts such as this. The Hebrew word is familiar to most people; it is *Torah*. Although *Torah* is a designation for the first part of the Hebrew Bible in traditional Jewish circles, it often (as here in Psalm 19) is bigger than the "thou shalts" and "thou shalt nots" of the Pentateuch (i.e. the first five books of Moses). *Torah* comes from a verb whose core connotation has to do with 'pointing out' or 'showing the way.' As a designation for the totality of Scripture, "law" pictures God's Word as showing His way to men. Therefore, here and in other places (e.g. throughout Psalm 119), it is better to translate this term by such English words as "instruction," "teaching," or "direction."

And what does this inscripturated divine direction for man's life accomplish? It has the innate ability to "turn" or "return" an individual. The term "soul" in scriptural context virtually never designates merely the metaphysical aspect of man's existence. It is a wholistic term according to the data of biblical anthropology, so, most frequently, it refers to the entire person. Furthermore, the key participle translated as "restoring" in the NASB and as "reviving" in the NIV, is wider in its applications. This causative verbal of which "the Law" is its subject comes from the primary word-group for repentance in the Old Testament. The Law of God characteristically has the ability to bring an unsaved sinner to repentance (i.e. "to turn" him salvifically) and "to return" (i.e. "revive") a straying believer.

Verse 7b goes on like this: "The testimony [i.e. the picture standing in the background of this word for the Word is one of the Scriptures *bearing witness* to their divine Author] of the LORD is trustworthy (or, faithful; or, reliable), making wise the simple." God's trustworthy testimonies have the ability to impart wisdom to any 'simple-minded one.' This axiom could be applied initially to salvation. Compare a historical reference to this kind of application in Paul's reminder to Timothy as found in 2 Timothy 3:15a: "and that from infancy you have known the sacred writings [largely, the Old Testament Scriptures at the time of Paul's writing] which are able [i.e. they have the ability, the power, the divine dynamic, etc.] to grant wisdom unto salvation . . ." [i.e."the wisdom that leads to salvation" (NASB)]. Notwithstanding, returning to Psalm 19:7b, it seems, because of the primary usage of the word "simple" as "open-minded" in Psalms, more of an emphasis is being placed on the crucial role of the Word in conveying its wisdom for life's ways to those who have already listened to God, but yet remain vulnerable in the area of making unwise ethical decisions.

Next v. 8a of Psalm 19 states: "The precepts [i.e. the words from the Word as God's "charges," "orders," etc.] are upright [i.e. ethically 'smooth' or 'on the level'], causing the heart to rejoice." These divine dictates are not burdensome, but contrastingly, they effectually mediate, to the core of a believer's being, the transcendent joy of the Lord.

In the last part of v. 8 the psalmist confirms these facts about the Word of God: "The commandment [usually appearing in the plural form "commands," i.e. various *orders* set up by God] of the Lord is pure (or, clean), enlightening the eyes." In view of the ethically blinded eyes of unbelievers and in recognition of episodes of moral near-sightedness on the part of believers, this is an especially vital function of God's Word. It can (i.e. it has the necessary power to) bring light to the eyes of the human heart. All such sample sufficiencies are divine gifts graciously given to us, who, left to ourselves, are devoid of the necessary dynamics for salvation and sanctification.

Now just before we move out of the Book of Psalms, it would be beneficial to revisit Psalm 119:93, this time paying special attention to the *means* that God uses to save. Again, the psalmist testifies therein: "I will never forget your precepts [i.e. the same word for the Word that appeared in Psalm 19:8a], because by them [i.e. *by means of* God's dynamic precepts] You [i.e. the LORD-God] gave me life." God habitually uses the efficient words from His Word both to impart spiritual life and to sustain that life.

Jeremiah employs some common images to picture the divine dynamic of the Word of God. I'd like to share three passages in reverse order of their appearance beginning with Jeremiah 23:29: "'Is not my word like fire,' declares the LORD, 'and like a hammer that breaks a rock in pieces?'" (NIV). These two similes depict the irresistible power of the Word of God. Its ability compares with the consuming burning of a fire and the action of a sledge which takes rocks and turns them into tiny fragments.

Now concerning the former imagery of fire, it previously occurred in some significant contexts. It was applied by the prophet to himself in Jeremiah 20:7ff., as he complained about his divine commissioning and resultant tough ministry. He was having such a rough time of it among the recalcitrant people to whom the LORD had sent him that he accused God of deceiving and bullying him. He wanted to quit, but he couldn't. Why? Because the dynamic of God's Word was powerfully affecting *him.* Listen to the implications of this truth in v. 9, "But if I should say, 'I will not remember Him [not an amnesia but a deliberate turning of the back to God] nor speak again in His name' [i.e. Jeremiah's thoughts of 'I quit!'], then it [i.e. the Word of God; cf. v. 8b] will be (or, becomes) like a consuming fire in my heart, (one) shut up in my bones; and I am weary of holding it in [i.e. 'I can't contain it!'] and I am not able" [i.e. 'I do not have the power to keep it in!']. Even in his own heart, Jeremiah could not suppress and stifle the Word's powerful operations. As painful as that was to the prophet personally, it was also good news for him; how much less could the recipients of God's oracles through him douse its fiery penetrations! With that in mind, listen to one more verse, Jeremiah 5:14: "Therefore, thus says the LORD, the God of hosts [or, "of armies"; a picture of the Divine Warrior], 'Because you [a plural form, vividly referring most immediately to false prophets] have spoken this word [with the force of 'after this manner'], behold [this marks the emphatic punch-line] I am making My words fire in your [a singular; i.e. Jeremiah's] mouth and this people wood, and it [i.e. the fire] will consume them." So the awesome power of the fire-Word can incinerate the wicked. But remember, it can also warm and melt down remnants of resistance in God's righteous ones.

Going to the New Testament, Paul's exuberant testimony in Romans 1:16 will provide a great launching pad; the apostle exclaims: "For I am not ashamed of the Gospel, for it is the power of God [in the Greek text the phrase "the power of God" is emphatically placed first in this explanatory clause about *why* the apostle is not ashamed of the Gospel] unto salvation in reference to every person who believes, to the Jew first and to the Gentile also." Paul's point in the second part of v. 16 is that the Gospel innately contains the power to generate salvation. The Greek word translated "power" here stands behind our English words "dynamic, dynamo, dynamite," etc. As a matter of fact, a participle from this word-group was noted earlier in a reference to Timothy's salvation in 2 Timothy 3:15 (i.e. the Scriptures *dynamically* bestowed the wisdom which led to his salvation). Furthermore, since this is *God's* power, it obviously carries with it all the dynamic of the Omnipotent One. So the Almighty uses the Gospel, i.e. His Word, as His dynamic for producing eternal results.

The powerful dynamic of the Gospel is conveyed by other images in Colossians 1:4-8. In these verses Paul lists some reasons for his thanksgiving to the Father (i.e. found in v. 3). He gives thanks because of the fidelity of the Colossians (v. 4) and, more importantly, because of the Gospel (vv. 5-8). He praises God especially for His Word's dynamic productivity in vv. 6b-8. Both the efficacy and the productivity of the Gospel are boldly highlighted in Paul's second observation of verse 6: "just as also in all the world it [i.e. the Gospel] is bearing fruit [most likely the middle form of this participle contextually bears dynamic force; contrast the same word, but in active form, applied to the Colossians in v. 10; i.e., this Gospel dynamically bears fruit in and of itself] and growing" [i.e. spreading]. So the Gospel's inherent dynamic is being noted and praised by Paul.

Paul not merely theologized about the Gospel's power, he also was quick to appropriate its dynamic and apply it throughout his own ministry. For example, by fully relying upon this sufficiency placed into his hands by God, he was privileged to observe the Lord effectually accomplishing eternal results in the many places where he had ministered the Gospel. A prime case in point involved the Thessalonians. First Thessalonians 1 summarizes how they had turned to God, and chapter 2, v. 13, provides some behind-the-scenes insights into their conversion. In a testimonial of praise, the apostle to the Gentiles says, "And on account of this we also are continually thanking God, because when you received the word of hearing from us, (that is the word) of God, you accepted (or, welcomed) it not [i.e. not merely] (as) a word of men but just as it truly is the word of God, which also effectually works in you, the ones who are believing." As you can tell from this attempt at a literal rendering of 1 Thessalonians 2:13, Paul's phrasing is quite choppy. However, whether translated more literally or more dynamically (cf., e.g., the NASB, and the NIV, etc.), the key points that Paul is making are crystal clear. By referring to God's Word which the Thessalonians had heard from Paul and company, he is emphasizing the *preached* Word. His phrasing, although stilted, traced, as it were, the Word of the Gospel from the receivers' end back through the channel of the communicators to its origin in God Himself. Then, when he adds the fact that this message was ultimately sourced in God, he links the dynamic efficacy of the Gospel with the words that he preached. As he proclaimed God's Word as a faithful mouth-piece of the Lord, he was conveying the very words of the Lord, words which carried with them all the divine dynamic necessary to save and to sanctify people. Furthermore, the omnipotently powerful dynamic which *effectually operates* on and in the hearts of sinners counteracts Satan's powerful operations for ill (cf., Ephesians 2:2 again, which uses a form of the same word-group).

So, when Paul spoke, God was speaking, because the apostle faithfully proclaimed the words from the Word.

Indeed, he carried on *God's business God's way*. As we are going to see later, in application to us ministerially, this is the only legitimate carry-over of 'apostolic succession' (cf., e.g., 2 Timothy 4:2ff. in Part III below).

Two quite familiar verses from the Epistle to the Hebrews make a significant contribution to the nuclear dynamic of the Word of God. In Hebrews 4:12-13 we find an intricate parallelism drawn between the Word of God (v. 12) and the God of the Word (v. 13). The primary reason "there is not a creature that is not exposed in His [i.e. God's] presence" and that "all things are naked and laid bare to Him, that is, to the One we must give an account" (v. 13), is that the infinitely powerful M. R. I. of His Word looks into every 'atom' of man's spiritual being. Indeed, using some terms and concepts that we have previously encountered, v. 12 affirms: "For the Word of God is living and effectual [this is an adjective of the same word-group that the verb "effectually operating" in 1 Thessalonians 2:13 came from] and sharper than any two-edged surgeon's scalpel [this word is usually translated "sword"; however, in the medical literature from ancient Greece, it referred to a double-edged scalpel, an image that seems to fit better into this context of the Great Physician doing sin surgery with His Word], even penetrating as far as a separation of soul and of spirit, of both joints and of marrow [representatives of the deepest center of man's being], even able to judge (or, to discern) reflections (or, deliberations) and thoughts of (the) heart." Notice structurally how v. 12 begins with affirmations about what the Word of God *is* followed by illustrations of what it can *do*, much like each line of Psalm 19:7-8. Also, conceptually notice how the last words of Hebrews 4:12 are similar to the words of Genesis 6:5 which spoke of "every formulation of the thoughts of the (human) heart" as being continually and exclusively evil. The Word of God is the divinely powerful x-ray machine that sees and exposes all spiritual motives and ethical malignancies. It is the powerful instrument which God has put into our hands to expose sin. Furthermore, the Bible is the Great Physician's 'scalpel' with which He performs spiritual 'heart transplants' (cf., e.g., Ezekiel 36:26). Why would any Christian servant engaged in any kind of ministry choose to resort to other ineffective means?

In James 1:18 is found a more generalized expression of the basic truth that the human author of Psalm 119:93 stated personally. Using new-birth imagery, James says, "Having willed, He [i.e. God] brought us forth by means of the Word of Truth [i.e. through the instrumentality of the Word of God] that we might be a kind of first fruits of His creatures." God effectually uses His Word to impart spiritual life; or phrasing it a little differently, His powerful birthing instrument is the Word. So, the same Word that exposed our terminal condition of sin also brought eternal life to us.

Peter chimes in like this in 1 Peter 1:23: "For you have been born again, not of perishable seed, but of imperishable, through the living and enduring word of God" (NIV). Peter, right up front, reminds his audience that they had not become regenerated out of any human source. Human "seed," operating according to the 'after-its-kind' principle (cf. e.g., John 1:13; 3:6 in its new birth context; etc.), cannot produce eternal life. Eternal life is sourced in God and mediated through His Word. Furthermore, as Peter notes at the end of v. 25, this life-giving Word was the *preached* word of the Gospel (cf. the preached Word that Paul noted had granted life to the Thessalonians). That same preached Word still has the divine dynamic to grant and to sustain spiritual life today.

Our Sufficiency 'in Heart'

As sketched out above, our in-hand weapon for war is propositional in nature. It is the dynamic Word of God inscripturated. But we have been blessed with an unseen personal 'Weapon,' the Spirit of God Himself. Obviously, we don't possess Him as in the sense of carrying Bibles with us. Nevertheless, we are to be dependent upon his Person for our lives and for our various ministries.

As a transition to this Personal Weapon, that is, the omnipotent dynamic that comes from the Spirit of God, a brief reconsideration of Ephesians 6:17 seems appropriate at this juncture. The final "piece" of the full amour of God is "the sword of the Spirit, which is the word (or, utterance) of God." My point here is that the Word of God which we do possess, has the Spirit of God as its divine Author. It is *His* sword that has been placed as a divinely mighty weapon into our hands. He wrote it (cf., e.g., 2 Peter 1:21), and ultimately, He wields it (cf., e.g., 1 Corinthians 2:10-13). It is as if, when we faithfully clutch its handle to use this sword in ministry, He personally places the power of His hand over ours.

Some Historical Emphases on this Sufficiency

Many early church fathers and all the great reformers taught how absolutely essential the Spirit's ministry was for salvation and sanctification. The Spirit of God, according to the New Testament, is explicitly the divine Agent of new birth. He is also the transcendent power Source of new life in Christ. These dogmas were accepted by all orthodox believers in the early church and thereafter.

When the Reformation came along, God used men like Luther, Calvin, and others to resuscitate the doctrines of sovereign grace. One of the doctrines they spent much time articulating more carefully was the *testimonium Spiritus Sancti* (Latin for the witness, or, secret testimony, of the Holy Spirit). Luther and Calvin wrote very extensively on this important subject. Calvin addressed the issue first. He was most concerned with the Holy Spirit's initial illumination of the Scriptures to any person God was drawing unto Himself (cf., e.g., the effectual call outlined in chapter 5). This inner witness of the Spirit involves, so to speak, the strategic 'third dimension' of divine persuasion added to the 'two-dimensional' words from the

Word that are being preached, read, etc. This supernaturally efficient witness speaks to the heart of the person convincing him that he is hearing the very words of God and persuasively applies these truths salvifically to his heart. Luther concurred with Calvin on this divine prerequisite for a person's salvation, but he also stressed the necessity of a follow-up ministry of illumination, not applied to salvation, of course, but applied to a believer's continuing study of the Word of God.

Some Biblical Expressions of this Sufficiency

In a context that exposes the inadequacy of man's knowledge when it comes to apprehending and applying spiritual truths, Paul revels in God's remedy outlined in 1 Corinthians 2:6-13. In this passage the apostle recognizes the Spirit to be the unique Conveyer of the truth. Historically, the Holy Spirit revealed truth to the apostolic circle (i.e. the primary thrust of vv. 6-10a; cf. also the *major* burden of John 14-16), but He is also the Teacher of truth to all believers. Back then He revealed truth to the apostolic circle as part of the process of divine inspiration, but subsequently He illumines truth for those who hear their words from the Word (cf., e.g., 12-13, 15-16). Of course, as we've already seen (cf. above in chapter 2), the unspiritual man is impervious to spiritual things (i.e. v. 14). The only way for him to understand and to welcome the spiritual things which bring spiritual life, is by the Spirit's operational dynamic of 1 Corinthians 2:10b-11 becoming effectual in his heart. So this great principle capsulized in one and a half verses must apply if illumination and salvation are to take place. Here is how that principle is proverbialized biblically: "For the Spirit searches all things, even the depths of God; for who from among men knows the things [in this context, most likely "thoughts"] of a [literally, the] man except the spirit of the man that is in him; so also the things [or again, probably "thoughts"] of God no person knows except the Spirit of God" (1 Corinthians 2:10b-11). Consequently, for any person to gain real knowledge about God, because of fallen man's hard-hearted resistance of spiritual things (Romans 1:18, 1 Corinthians 2:14, etc.), the Spirit of God must crash through in His unique role as Truth Conveyor and Persuader.

In the process of conveying the truths of the Word, the Spirit initially convicts. For example, Christ said this of Him in John 16:8: "And when the One [i.e. the *Paraclete* (v. 7), the Holy Spirit pictured as Helper, Advocate, etc.] comes, He will convict (or, expose; or, blame; or, convince) the world concerning sin and concerning righteousness and concerning judgment." Only the Spirit of God can convince a resistant unbeliever (cf. v. 9) that he is a sinner. Only by His sovereign and efficient operations on resistant hearts does conviction come.

Then conviction leads to conversion. His persuasive power concerning sin becomes His productive power concerning salvation. The Spirit is the hands-on Agent of regeneration. Nicodemus had to be reminded of this reality in John, chapter 3. Incidentally regeneration was not a new 'invention' for the New Testament era. Although the language and images were different, the necessity of regeneration for Old Testament saints to be Old Testament saints was always a clear inference theologically (cf., e.g., Christ's indictment of Nicodemus in John 3:10). As Christ reviewed God's powerful work of the new birth for the enlightenment of Nicodemus, our Lord reminded him that it takes more than physical birth to enter the kingdom. Since finite and fallen people can only produce that which is finite and fallen (i.e. v. 6a), it takes the Spirit of God to produce a product of God (v. 6b). This is why it is absolutely necessary that the person be born again (v. 7). And there is only one Source of new birth, the Spirit of God (cf. the rolling repetitions of the phrase "of the Spirit" in vv. 5, 6, and 8).

So the Holy Spirit's effectual working with His Word is the only weaponry capable of convicting and converting rebellious people. Furthermore, the dynamic operations of these divine efficacies do not cease at the time of regeneration. By God's grace, the same sufficiencies continue throughout the process of sanctification. Because of sin's remnants and restrictions, we need to remain dependent upon the resources of God's Spirit and His Word in order "to keep on growing in the grace and knowledge of our Lord and Savior, Jesus Christ" (2 Peter 3:18).

Take, for example, once again, the author of Psalm 119. I've already shown from v. 93 that he had been totally dependent upon the sufficiencies of the Person of God and the precepts of God for salvation and sanctification. That dependent attitude and outlook did not change throughout his walk with God. Every student of Psalm 119 recognizes that the Psalmist's remarkable maturity as a disciple had a lot to do with his Word dependence. However, maturity from the Word did not come mechanistically. Indeed, all of his pleas to God exhibit another dynamic that stood behind this disciple's growth and development. Through prayer, a very conspicuous characteristic of any dependent disciple, the author of Psalm 119 made headway in holy living.

Quite often, he broadcasts his reliance upon these twin resources in stereo. He prays to God to effectuate the Word that he was diligently studying for the purpose of moral maturity. Compare, for example, "Uncover my eyes, then I will behold wonderful things out of Your Law" (v. 18); "Teach me, O LORD, the way of [i.e. not just the Word, but the Word applied to the ways of his life] your statutes, so that I may observe it to the end [i.e. to the end of his life]. Grant me understanding [one of the primary Old Testament terms for the practical wisdom that is needed to survive life's challenging highways and by-ways], so that I may observe Your Law and keep it wholeheartedly" (vv. 33-34); "The unfolding of your words gives light, giving understanding to the simple. . . . Establish my footsteps by means of your word, and do not let any iniquity have dominion over me" (vv. 130-133); etc.

Another good example of the seen and unseen divine sufficiencies at work in people may be found in a passage that I referred to previously, 1 Thessalonians 1. We looked particularly at the efficacy of the preached Word at work in 1 Thessalonians 2:13 and noted how it provided theological background for the quite rapid and radical conversion of the Thessalonians as chronicled in chapter 1. But right in the middle of 1 Thessalonians 1 is another important Pauline explanation as to how their wondrous 180° turn around for God had come about. He attributes their conversion to the powerful workings of the Spirit with His Word as scriptural utterances came forth out of the mouths of the Lord's servants: "our Gospel did not come to you in word only [i.e. not merely as human words proceeding out of human mouths] but also in power [i.e. the divine *dynamic* returns] and in the Holy Spirit and with much full assurance (or, certainty)" (1 Thessalonians 1:5a). The Spirit of God powerfully works with the dynamic Word of God persuading formerly rebellious and resistant hearts of the life-giving truth of the Gospel. This divine weaponry alone can produce spiritual results for eternity. And we must faithfully and consistently appropriate and rely on these divine sufficiencies if we are to do *God's Business God's way.*

Part III

Sharing
And
Serving

At the core of the Great Commission lies discipleship; therefore, we must be about its two primary concerns, sharing with the lost (i.e. evangelism) and serving the Body (i.e. edification). But, by now, it should have become obvious that *how* we carry on Christ's business is of paramount importance. Relying on rhetoric and/or reason will never produce eternal results. We do not have the innate resources to mouth- and mind-wrestle anyone into the kingdom, no matter how eloquent and astute we may seem to be. Nor, relying on our own resources, do we even have the capacity to turn around a brother or sister who is erring. In whatever kind of sinning scenario he or she may be involved in at a given time, that person is likely to be very resistant. He or she won't be 'reasonable.' The bull-headedness of sin's hangover is a formidable foe, also calling for our utter dependence upon the divine resources when dealing with such professing 'family' members. And don't forget that the subtleties of sin have a tendency to draw *us* away from our true sufficiencies. All too often, our pride manifests itself while 'ministering,' cutting us off from God's power.

With these thoughts constantly in mind, it is time to put the capstone on our building project. I'd like to construct it by referring to scriptural models which corroborate a basic biblical methodology for ministry. Then I'd like to add to it some inferential 'how-to' suggestions.

Chapter 7
Scriptural Models
For Ministry

"Thus Saith the LORD" Models

As the prophets, and later, the apostles were com-missioned and sent out to the front lines their battle cry was to be "Thus saith the LORD." It would be advantageous to survey all the many introductory formulas of the Bible and their basic significance. However, a few representative formulas and texts will suffice for an accurate picture of the whole.

A good place to begin is with the LORD's commissioning of Ezekiel (Ezekiel 1-3). Listen carefully to the following excerpts from these opening chapters:

> Then He [i.e. the LORD; cf. His descriptions via the vision of chapter 1] said to me, "Son of man, stand on your feet that I may speak with you!" (2:1). And as He spoke to me the Spirit entered me and set me on my feet; and I heard *Him* speaking to me (2:2). Then He said to me, "Son of man, I am sending you to the sons of Israel, to a rebellious people who have rebelled against Me; they and their fathers have transgressed against Me to this very day [installment #1 of a refresher course on sin as rebellious resistance] (2.3). And I am sending you to them who are stubborn and obstinate children [installment #2: 'Remember, Ezekiel, they are tough-faced and heard-hearted!']; and you shall say to them, 'Thus says the Lord God' [i.e. the Sovereign LORD] (2:4). As for them, whether they listen or not [i.e. 'Don't

concern yourself with results; that's My business!']—for they are a rebellious house [installment #3]—they will know that a prophet has been among them [How? By ministering only with God's authoritative words!] (2:5). . . . But you shall speak My words [i.e. 'The content of all your communications must be restricted to *My* words'] to them whether they listen or not, for they are rebellious" [installment #5; #4 came at the end of v. 6] (2:7). . . . Then He said to me, "Son of man, go to the house of Israel and speak with My words to them" [i.e. 'only *by means of* my words are you to engage them'] (3:4). . . . Moreover, He said to me, "Son of man, take into your heart all My words which I shall speak to you [i.e. 'let My words affect you in the core of your being before you pass them on to the nation!'], and listen closely (3:10). And go to the exiles, to the sons of your people, and speak to them and tell them, whether they listen or not: 'Thus says the Lord God' [i.e. this is not a broken record; 'Ezekiel, you must do *My business My way*!] (3:11). . . . I will make your tongue stick to the roof of your mouth so that you will be dumb, and cannot be a man who rebukes them [i.e. 'You have no business speaking on your own initiative relying on your own inadequate resources; puny, natural resources can do nothing except possibly catalyze the hearers' prideful resistance; any real change calls for the supernatural dynamics of the Spirit working with My words'], for they are a rebellious house [installment #?—lost count of them all!] (3:26). But when I speak to you, I will open your mouth, and you will say to them, 'Thus says the Lord God.' He who hears, let him hear; and he who refuses, let him refuse [i.e. again, 'You be faithful *to do My busi-*

ness My way, and I'll take care of the different kinds of results!] for they are a rebellious house" [i.e. one more time for God's good measure] (v. 27) (Ezekiel 2:1-5, 7; 3:4, 10-11, 26-27, NASB).

Ezekiel's task was to be faithful by taking sin seriously, by sticking to the Word of God as commanded, by communicating it accurately with 'two-dimensional' clarity, and by dependently relying upon God to accomplish whatever He desires in the inner ear of the heart of the prophet's audience.

In Chapter 1, I pointed out the significance of Romans 3:9-20 as the climax to Paul's first major section of that great epistle dealing with the Gospel of God's sovereign grace. His carefully knit arguments of 1:18ff. reveal the universal condemnation of the race. It is *how* he brings these arguments to a head that is of special methodological interest here. If you will, the *coupes de grace* of Paul's climax is found in the citations of Scripture contained in Romans 3:10b-18 (for some comments, cf. Chapter 1 above under the discussion about "Man's Perpetual Resistance"). The formula that he uses to introduce this chain of Old Testament references is a very important one in the New Testament; here it reads: "Just as, (or, even as) it is written." The verb "it is written" comes from the same Greek word-group as the noun for the "Scriptures," and its form conveys the following sense: 'it was originally inscripturated with full divine authority back then, and it continues to retain its original authority and applicability.' So, Paul, an apostle of our Lord Jesus Christ with full authority in all of his proclamations to the Church, was not reluctant, but was always ready, to appeal to the inscripturated authority of God's Word. How much more should we!

In 1 Corinthians 15:1-4 Paul employs another introductory formula, two out of three times, as he presents the basic essentials of the Gospel of Christ. Using the language of *true* tradition in 1 Corinthians 15:1-3a, Paul reminds his audience how he had received this tradition from Christ, passed it on to them, and how they in turn had received it from him. This was the *good* tradition (as opposed to the false tradition sourced in men; cf., e.g., Mark 7 again) of the Good News, the essentials of which he outlines in vv. 3b-4: "that Christ (or, Messiah) died on behalf of our sins according to [i.e. a preposition that often appeals to a norm or standard; i.e. 'in accordance with,' 'on the basis of,' etc.] the Scriptures and that He was buried and that He was raised on the third day according to the Scriptures." Although the major function of Paul and the other apostles, as eye-witnesses of Christ's resurrection, was to publish the evidences [i.e. a task divinely restricted to those eye-witnesses] that Jesus was the Messiah, they did not, nor could not, do this in a vacuum. They had to begin with the authoritative Old Testament references which predicted the death, burial, and resurrection of Christ. And this they did with full reliance upon the Old Testament Scriptures.

This particular prophetic-apostolic precedent, unlike virtually all the rest of their unique prerogatives, is to be passed on to those who followed them. Peter applies this precedent of relying unreservedly on God's authoritative Word to second generation Christians when he writes: "If anyone speaks, he should do it as one speaking the very words of God" (1 Peter 4:11a, NIV). The implication is that whenever we open our mouths in ministry of any kind, we should confidently communicate *what God has said*. Indeed, the second part of this verse is a corollary; we must be absolutely dependent upon God and His resources at all times: "If anyone serves, he should do it with the strength God provides [especially since on our own we are feeble and frail], so that in all things God may be praised through Jesus Christ. To him be the glory and the power for ever and ever. Amen" (1 Peter 4:11b, NIV). Note carefully that these axiomatic scenarios for service were so important to Peter that he had to interrupt his instructions with an appropriate doxology.

Models from a Couple
of Reformations

Two of the greatest revivals of Old Testament history were respectively the one under King Josiah and the one during the post-exilic period under Ezra-Nehemiah. Concerning the one under Josiah, prior to his becoming king there had been gross idolatry in Judah for nearly sixty years under the wicked reigns of Manasseh and Amon. After Amon's servants killed him, his son Josiah, became king at the tender age of eight. The LORD providentially prepared this so-called boy-king to serve Him. The LORD brought out from 'their closets' some apparently faithful religious leaders. These people undoubtedly had significant impact on the young Josiah, of whom the prophetic historian says, "and he did right in the sight of the LORD and walked in all the way of his father [i.e. ancestor] David, nor did he turn aside to the right or to the left" (2 Kings 22:2, NASB).

In the process of trying to repair and restore the temple which had fallen into misuse and disuse under the previous idolatrous regimes (cf. vv. 3-7 of 2 Kings 22), Hilkiah the high priest had unearthed a scroll from the Old Testament Scriptures. Second Kings 22:8 records this joyous finding: "Then Hilkiah the high priest said to Shaphan the scribe, 'I have found the book of the law in the house of the LORD,' and Hilkiah gave the book to Shaphan who read it" (NASB). Excitedly, Shaphan brought it to the king. And immediately upon bringing it to the king, the account affirms that "Shaphan read it in the presence of the king. And it came about when the king heard the words of the book of the law, that he tore his clothes" (2 Kings 22:10b-11). The tearing of the clothes was the king's outward indication of some significant inward response. As a matter of fact, when the king sent Hilkiah, Shaphan and others to seek an applicational clarification from the LORD about what these words from His Word would hold for Judah, the Prophetess Huldah said this about King Josiah:

> But to the king of Judah who sent you to in-
> quire of the LORD thus you shall say to him,
> "Thus says the LORD God of Israel, '*Regarding*
> the words which you have heard, because your
> heart was tender and you humbled yourself
> before the LORD when you heard what I spoke
> against this place and against its inhabitants
> that they should become a desolation and a
> curse [the scroll which had been found and
> read likely contained some of the curses from
> Deuteronomy about God's judgment of a dis-
> obedient nation], and you have torn your
> clothes and wept before Me, I have truly heard
> you,' declares the LORD" (2 Kings 22:18-19,
> NASB).

She also informed the messengers that because of the king's response to God's Word the LORD would not bring this great judgment [i.e. the forthcoming captivity in Babylon] upon them until after Josiah would pass off the scene. But all of that to ask this, What prompted the king to repent? It was God's effectuation of the words from His Word which had been "read" to Josiah (cf. again, "read" and "heard" in vv. 10-11). No wonder Paul commanded young Timothy in a church context: "Until I come, keep on devoting yourself to the public reading (of the Scriptures) . . ." (1 Timothy 4:13a).

Now the story of King Josiah is not over. He was not content with his individual pardon whereby his subjects would merely reap second-hand benefits from his per-sonal repentance. So, he summoned the leaders of Judah along with all the people of Jerusalem and Judah, to the temple, and there he personally read the scroll to them (cf. 2 Kings 23:1-2). After that, it recounts that "the king stood by the pillar and made a covenant before the LORD, to walk after the LORD, and to keep His com-mandments and His testimonies and His statutes with all *his* heart and all *his* soul, to carry out the words of this covenant that were written in this book. And all the people entered into the covenant" (2 Kings 23:3, NASB). In days subsequent to that covenant which had been precipitated by the reading and hearing of the Word of the LORD, marvelous fruits of repentance were displayed throughout the kingdom (cf. 2 Kings 23:4ff. and 2 Chronicles 34:32-35:19). What a remarkable turn-around had occurred, especially in comparison with the horrendously evil days of Josiah's predecessors, and it was all set in motion and brought to pass by the dynamics of a portion of the Old Testament Scriptures read in the hearing of the people.

About 200 years later according to Old Testament history, the reading *and* the textual exposition of the Word of God precipitated another awesome reformation, the account of which is recorded in Nehemiah 8-13. Chapter 8 emphasizes the launching pad for it. After the people were assembled in Jerusalem inside the "Water Gate," "they asked Ezra the scribe to bring the book of the Law of Moses which the LORD had commanded Israel" (Nehemiah 8:1). On this occasion in the presence of the men, the women, and their children with capacity to understand, he read from the Word of God for six hours (Nehemiah 8:2-3). Furthermore, Ezra apparently had his associates distributed among the people, and in conjunction with his reading from the Hebrew scrolls, these men were "causing" the people "to understand," that is, they were expounding and explaining the words from God's Word (v. 7). Verse 8 clarifies this process a little more: "Now they read from the book of the Law of God [i.e. here described by its ultimate Source; cf. "The Law of Moses" back in v. 1], translating it (and/or) making it clear (or, making it distinct), even making it comprehensible so that they understood the reading." The optional renderings of "translating" and "making clear" (i.e. explaining and expounding) each have credible support standing behind them. As a illustration of this fact, concerning the former rendering note the text of NASB and the margin of NIV, and concerning the latter, see the text of NIV and the marginal reading of NASB! As a matter of fact, I feel that both of these activities might have been going on. Historically remember that the people had been in captivity for a long time, in a land that spoke Aramaic (i.e. their Hebrew had probably gotten very rusty!). These men at first may have had to paraphrase the Hebrew text into Aramaic in order to continue to explain it clearly. But also, contextually there seems to be a significant emphasis on exposition (cf., e.g., the major thrust of the participle in v. 7; indeed some rabbinical tradition paraphrases this activity as "they expounded the text"). But the bottom line is that when the people heard the words from the Word of God so faithfully and carefully conveyed to them, the result was not only comprehension (v. 8b) but also contrition (v. 9b). This deep conviction brought about by the clear communication of the Scriptures led to a joyous celebration of a holy day (vv. 10-12).

But that's not the end of this story. In Nehemiah 8:13ff. it continues with another gathering, this time of the family elders and religious leaders. These men gathered to Ezra for the purpose of gaining more insight from the words of the Law (v. 13). When they heard about the commandments concerning the Feast of Booths (v. 14; cf., e.g., Leviticus 23:34), they ordered that this week-long commemoration be observed throughout the land (v. 15), and so it was (vv. 16-17).

During this time Ezra kept on ministering the Word of God (v. 18). Then the people assembled for more reading and hearing of the Word of God (Nehemiah 9:3a). The power of the communicated words from God's Law generated widespread conviction and confession (Nehemiah 9:2b, 3b). This immediately produced verbal worship and practical worship (Nehemiah 9:4ff.). The Word of God, read and expounded, was powerfully sufficient both in its exposure of sin and its energizing of sanctification.

Our Lord's Model

Christ's model for ministry is especially striking in that He was *God* in flesh. And yet, during His First Advent, He carried on His ministries by the same resources He has made available to us. Indeed, right after His baptism, which symbolically inaugurated His public ministry, we are introduced to the resources upon which He relied during the kenosis, the Personal and propositional sufficiencies respectively of the Spirit of God and the Word of God (cf. Chapter 6). These divine resources are conspicuously observable in His first challenge, a three round bout with Satan the archenemy (cf. Matthew 4:1-11; Mark 1:12-13; Luke 4:1-13). The account in Matthew begins with some crucial background information in the first two verses of chapter 4. However, verse 1 is most significant in that it affirms that Jesus "was led up by the Spirit into the desert to be tempted by the devil" (Matthew 4:1). Mark's language is even more vivid, "the Spirit drove Him out [i.e. sent Him out] into the wilderness" (Mark 1:12). Indeed, Jesus, being "full of the Holy Spirit" (Luke 4:1), was submissive to God's leading.

Furthermore, as Satan dangled three baited barbs before Him, Jesus responded each time with an appeal to the authority of God's Word (Matthew 4:4, 7, 10). In all three of our Lord's scriptural sword thrusts, the introductory formula was "it is written," that is, the formula which asserts the original passage's divine authority along with its appropriate application to the current situation. After Jesus did not deviate from these divine dynamics, the devil departed (Matthew 4:11) for the time being (Luke 4:13).

Many times during Christ's public career, the devil sent his earthly henchmen after Him. The archenemy usually chose the hypocritical religious leaders of the day to assist him (remember Christ's identification of them in John 8:44). Their challenges of Jesus escalated as His ministry was approaching its final goal. For example, in an unholy alliance of people who were normally religious opponents, the Sadducees and the Pharisees 'tag-teamed' our Lord in Matthew 22. First, Christ responded to the wickedly motivated case-scenario proposed by the Sadducees who did not believe in the resurrection (cf. Matthew 22:23-33). He did not respond with the complicated reasonings of the rabbis, but with one example from the Scriptures. His succinct rebuttal is solidly based upon the present tense significance of God's statement to Moses in Exodus 3:6 (cf. Matthew 22:32). That appeal to God's Word not only silenced them, but also caused the audience to buzz.

Then came the Pharisees who sent a Mosaic 'theologian' up against Jesus. He wanted to trap our Lord with his questions (Matthew 22:36); however, Jesus responded to his question clearly and concisely from the Word of God. Then it was time for 'turn-about,' and Jesus put the Pharisees on the horns of a dilemma asking them about whose Son the Messiah was, David's or Yahweh's (Matthew 22:42). Although, according to the flesh, He was geneologically David's Son, He was God's unique Son both eternally and incarnationally. To make this latter point Jesus cites David, quoting Psalm 110:1. Then resting on this divinely authoritative answer from the Old Testament Scriptures, which can't be broken (cf. Jesus summary affirmation of the significance of the authority of the Bible in John 10:35), He simply concludes, "'If David then calls Him "Lord," how is He his son?'" (Matthew 22:45, NASB). Our Lord's consistent employment of God's Word as the final court of appeal in all situations once again silenced these cunning opponents (Matthew 22:46). This propositional resource, the Word of God, has the divine dynamic to end counterproductive dialogues and debates.

To round off Jesus' model for ministry, a post-resurrection episode seems fitting. In Luke 24 Jesus reproved the two on the road to Emmaus, then later He lovingly illuminated the men whom He had previously commissioned as apostles. In each case what finally got through to these various people was the Word of God explained. The two men traveling back to Emmaus after the events of Passion Week were representative of Christ's "disciples" after our Lord's crucifixion; they were confused and disappointed. Although privy to the report of the women (Luke 24:22-23), like the apostles (Luke 24:11), they were unwilling to believe what Christ had been teaching His flock for about a year (i.e. about His death, burial, *and resurrection*; cf., e.g. Matthew 16:21). Therefore, Jesus forcefully reprimanded them with these words: "O foolish ones and slow in heart [the hangover of the heart returns again with its paralyzing effects] to believe on all that the prophets spoke!" (v. 25). They had obviously picked out the deliverance promises of Christ's coming, especially the political ones (cf. v. 21a), and ignored the fact that Messiah would have to take care of the people's sin problem first. Therefore, Jesus continues with these words: "'Was it not necessary for the Christ to suffer these things and to enter into His glory?'" (v. 26, NASB). Then Luke summarizes probably the greatest message ever preached, noting: "and beginning with Moses and all the Prophets, he explained to them what was said in all the Scriptures concerning himself" (v. 27, NIV). Our Lord likely emphasized the passion prophecies of the Old Testament (like Psalms 16:10; 22:1; Isaiah 53; etc.). Jesus' method is capsulized in the word "explained." The Greek word-group from which this verb comes shows up in our English word "hermeneutics"; Christ may be pictured here as doing 'hermeneutics' on these Old Testament passages. He was carefully interpreting and expounding them. After He had done so, and after they had stopped in a village for supper and He had broken bread with them and blessed it (vv. 28-30), "their eyes were opened [i.e. the skeptically dull eyes of their heart] and they recognized Him" (v. 31a, b, NASB). Then He disappeared. As soon as that happened, they began to converse with one another, and their testimony was the same. What they said practically confirmed the method of Jesus (cf. v. 27): "Was not our heart burning [i.e. were not our hearts resultantly on fire] in us while (or, as) [i.e. this pin-points the coordinate time of the melting of their hard-hearted resistance] He was speaking to us on the road, while (or, as) [again identifying the time and occasion of their conviction] He opened up the Scriptures for us" (v. 32). It is interesting that the "opening up" of the Scriptures is that which God uses to open up the doors of the heart (this is the same verb that was used to describe Lydia's conversion in Acts 16:14; later, I'll mention it in connection with Paul's methodology as noted by Luke in Acts 17:3). The fiery dynamic of God's Word (cf. Jeremiah 23:29 again) is more than sufficient both to convict and to convert. Jesus not only knew this, but also never deviated from a consistent ministerial application of this reality.

As we move on to the last part of Luke 24, we read about how Christ 'woke up' the skeptical apostles (remember their condemning attitude in v. 11). Now the two on the road to Emmaus had gone back to Jerusalem (uphill no less!) late that night, and they were telling the apostles what had just happened to them (vv. 33-35). As they were speaking, Christ appeared in the midst of all of them (v. 36). They reacted fearfully, but Jesus calmed them down, even eating something to allay their thoughts of a ghost (vv. 37-43). Then, very importantly, using the same basic method He had used earlier that evening with the two, Christ pulled the mighty Sword of the Spirit out (v. 44) and "opened up [i.e. the same verb that appeared in v. 32; cf. Acts 16:14; etc.] their mind [to counteract noetic hangover] so that they might understand (or, spiritually comprehend) the Scriptures" (v. 45). The illuminated Word of God fully and finally accomplished what all the evidences were unable to do. Now that the credibility of the essentials of the Gospel was settled in the hearts of Christ's apostles, they would be ready to go forth with its message after Pentecost (vv. 46-49).

Models from the Book of Acts

Invalid Contructs

Since the Book of Acts is a record of the growth of Christ's church in its infancy, many Christians feel that *any* precedent found in it may or even must be carried over into our contemporary methodologies and/or practices. For example, most charismatics base much of their theology on *what* the early church did. Generally speaking, not much attention is paid to certain theological qualifications as to *why* they did what they did.

But let's focus on this theologically naive tendency in association with methodology for ministry. A good portion of the modern church asserts or assumes that we are to be 'Acts-kinds' of "witnesses" employing evidences in a similar manner as the apostolic circle did. However, when Christ said to the apostles that they were to be witnesses, He meant first-hand *eye-witnesses* (cf., e.g., the account we just left, especially plugging v. 48 back into their having witnessed Christ's passion and resurrection in v. 46). Luke, the author of the gospel bearing his name and of Acts, is crystal clear on this concept of witness. He even records Peter's rehearsal of the special prerequisites for an eye-witness apostle in Acts 1:21-22. As a matter of fact, if one carefully traces the "you" of "you are my witnesses" in Acts 1:8 back through the 'these's' 'they's' and 'them's' of vv. 3-7, the specific target group of these particular marching orders was the apostolic circle (v. 2). This does not mean that the contemporary believer is not to be a 'witness' in the sense of carrying out the Great Commission of Matthew 28:19-20 (although the word "witness" is avoided in these much more broadly applied marching orders). We Christians today, therefore, could be called third-rank witnesses; we are commanded to disciplize but certainly not be *the* primary "Witness" (that task belongs uniquely to the Spirit; cf. John 14-16) nor to be apostolic-circle eye-witnesses. Much doctrinal data could be brought to bear on this unique function of the apostles; however, I would like to point the reader in the direction of a few biblical illustrations that show how this worked out in the early church. Concerning eye-witnesses ministering to second generation Christians, or potential second generation Christians, note how the "we's" of the eye-witness apostles carefully differentiated them from the "you's" of the recipients in passages such as Acts 10:39-43; 1 Corinthians 15:1-11; 1 John 1:1-3; etc.

Those of the apostolic circle were eye-witnesses, so one of their primary tasks was to present the "evidences" that Jesus was the Messiah predicted in the Old Testament Scriptures. In their preaching and their writings they were called upon by the Lord through His special commissioning of them to demonstrate that He was indeed the promised One. This is illustrated in Luke's comment about Paul in Acts 17:2-3: "And according to Paul's custom, he went to them, and for three Sabbaths reasoned [i.e. in its first-century synagogue setting this word connoted 'to deliver a discourse'; cf. 'preaching a sermon'] with them from the Scriptures [i.e. his authoritative resource], explaining [this is that "opening up" term again (cf. Luke 24:32, 45); i.e. he was expounding those Old Testament passages] and giving evidence [i.e. he 'placed before' them the historical facts that pointed to Jesus being the Messiah who was predicted in the Old Testament; in other words, he was doing exactly what a New Testament apostle was supposed to do] that the Christ [i.e. Messiah] had to suffer and rise again from the dead, and *saying,* 'This Jesus whom I am proclaiming to you is the Christ'" [i.e. Messiah] (NASB). Paul's giving of evidence was far different from the 'precedent' supposedly derived from it by contemporary ministers who advocate an unbridled employment of all kinds of so-called evidentialist arguments. Yet, in ministry, we do pass along the now *inscripturated* eye-witness evidences from the hand of the apostolic circle. We have both testaments in our possession today. Consequently, our resource is not some insufficient combination of so-called 'evidenc-

es' and arguments, but the complete, powerfully sufficient Word of God. The Scriptures alone must ever remain the footing, foundation, and superstructure both for
our method and for our ministry.

While we're still in Acts 17, I need to mention one
more invalid construct which comes from an eccentric
understanding of Paul's method reflected in vv. 16ff. This
passage is a recorded 'first' in the history of the early
church. Although "Paul's custom" was to enter the synagogues wherever he went and to expound explicit Messi-
anic prophecies from the Old Testament showing how
Jesus fulfilled them (cf. again Acts 17:2-3), Luke draws attention for the first time to another setting for the apostle's Gospel ministry, "the market place." This was
Athens' 'mall', a place not only where things were bought
and sold and legal business was transacted, but also
where the philosophers and debaters 'hung out' (cf. especially Luke's parenthetical comment in v. 21). Representatives from Greece's major philosophical 'schools' also
hung out there, undoubtedly for the purpose of engaging
in intellectual 'jousting tournaments' (cf. v. 18a). In other
words, this setting for Paul's ministry was one of encoun-
tering 'raw' Gentiles, many of whom were of the worse
variety, arrogant intellectuals filled with the counterfeit
wisdom of the world.

Now how could or would he communicate the Good
News to this kind of constituency? By expositions of
chapter-and-verse from the Old Testament Scriptures?
Not at the outset anyway. At this point is where some
modern reconstructors of Paul's methodology assume
that Paul was willing to compromise both his communication and his content for the sake of meeting them on
'their own turf.' In so doing, they open up a wide door to
'going about' God's business *man's* way! Other modern
methodologists say that Paul did do this in a desperate
attempt 'to reach them' but realized later that he was
wrong. These scenario builders assume that because Paul
failed in this attempt [but he really didn't; cf. v. 34], he

later 'confessed his sins' in 1 Corinthians 2:1-5. However, neither of these interpretations of Acts 17:16ff. is accurate. Therefore, such hypothetical scenarios of what Paul had supposedly done in Acts 17 cannot be regarded as models for our ministry.

Right from the start, the "apostle to the Gentiles," "the bond-slave of Christ," was straightforward with the essentials of the Gospel. He proclaimed the Person and work of Christ. For example, Luke emphasizes the fact that even in the mall of Athens, "he was preaching [i.e. 'an on-going *proclamation* of the Good News'] Jesus and the resurrection" (v. 18). There is not a shred of compromise here concerning both his message and his method. However, the arrogant philosophers upon hearing the heart of the Gospel message accused him of being a "seed-picker," a gutter-sparrow kind of philosopher who picked up scraps from here and there. Why did they respond like that? Well, in their 'great brilliance' and based upon their polytheistic background (cf., e.g., vv. 16-23), as Paul spoke to them, obviously in Greek, they interpreted him as arguing for two new deities, a male deity "Jesus" and his consort female deity '*Anastasis.*' They assumed that *anastasis* was a woman's name and not to be translated as "resurrection." Furthermore, they would be 'naturally' driven to that conclusion because virtually all Greeks refused to entertain the idea of the resurrection of the body (cf. the subsequent reaction of many of them in v. 32). To them the "body" was bad, but the "spirit" was good. They even had a little saying that rhymed in Greek *sōma sēma*, "the body is a tomb." Consequently, the concept of the *resurrected* Jesus, a central tenant of the true Gospel, would be repugnant in the estimation of these arrogant intellectuals.

Because of that encounter in the market place, Paul was brought to the Hill of Ares, the Greek god of war (vv. 19, 22). By this time, the apostle was obviously beginning to understand how difficult it was to share the Good-News message with people who carried along with them this kind of 'baggage.' So, did he now compromise his content in the presence of these "'intellectuals'" as he was invited to clarify what he had been preaching in the mall? No, but he did need to package the fundamental truths about God differently from his expositions in synagogues of Jewish and proselyte constituencies. Therefore, communicating carefully and wisely, he moved from where they were as atheists, standing accountable in the presence of the only true God who is the Creator and who rules sovereignly over all (cf. vv. 22-29), to their need for repentance in view of the reality of a coming day of judgment. Furthermore, this one and only true God had predetermined that His Son Jesus whom He raised from the dead was to sit on that awesome throne of reckoning. Although Luke does not say it, the implication is that this mentioning of the resurrected Christ stopped Paul's message short. Nevertheless, he had communicated basic biblical truths to them, and as I already pointed out, the apostle's method here must not be characterized as a total failure (cf. again v. 34). So, under exceedingly challenging circumstances, he still had done *God's business God's way.*

Valid Continuities

Clear examples of early Christians from the Book of Acts ministering dependently by unreservedly relying on the sufficiencies of God surface on nearly every page of its inspired, historical annals. Again, I'll select a few illustrative examples. In Acts 8:26-40 is found the account of the Ethiopian eunuch and Philip. Philip was divinely sent to catch up to this court official who was returning to his home after a pilgrimage to worship in Jerusalem. The eunuch had probably become a Jewish proselyte, not only because he had made a trip to Jerusalem but also because he was studying a scroll of Isaiah when Philip caught up to him (v. 28). In the sovereign timing of God, he was reading from Isaiah 53 (cf. Acts 8:32-33). His problem was that (understandably) he couldn't figure out from the context of this great 'Servant Song' of Isaiah who the prophet was talking about. Philip's response to the eunuch's perplexity and question (vv. 30-31, 34) is recorded in v. 35, a verse that contains the methodological punch-line of this passage: "and Philip, opening up his mouth [i.e. an idiom normally indicating that an important message is to follow; cf., e.g., Matthew 5:2; Acts 10:34; etc.] and beginning from this Scripture [remember the similar procedure of our Lord in Luke 24:27], preached [i.e. the Good-News verb] Jesus to him." No fancy language or frilly arguments; building upon that solid Old Testament foundation, Philip simply announced the Good News to this man from Ethiopia. That God was pleased to work in the eunuch's heart and to save him is confirmed by his responses (cf. vv. 36-40).

At this juncture it may prove beneficial to return to Acts 10, the account of Peter preaching the Gospel to those gathered in Cornelius' house. Since Cornelius is called a "devout man and one who feared God" by Luke (v. 2), it can be safely assumed that he was a Jewish proselyte. This meant that Peter could address this man and those of his household with an understanding that they were basically familiar with the Old Testament Scriptures. So, after both Cornelius and Peter responded to their respective divine invitations and had come together by divine appointment (vv. 3-33), the apostle heralded the Good News (i.e. vv. 34-43). His message seemed to capsulize the major milestones of Jesus' public ministry as recorded in the Gospels. It is possible in view of Luke's comment at the beginning of v. 44 (i.e. "while Peter was still [or, yet] speaking these things") that Peter planned to give more data or to clarify what he had already told them, but such a conclusion is not necessarily demanded. God, through the words of Peter's Gospel message was pleased to grant them life (vv. 44-48; . . . remember also, Acts 11:1-18).

Acts 18:24-28 contains a very interesting illustration of *doing God's business God's way*. It is interesting not just on account of the main character, Apollos, but also in view of his basic methodology not changing after being brought 'up to speed' on the Person and work of Christ (cf. vv. 25-26). The man behind the method is described in v. 24: "Now a certain Jew whose name was Apollos [cf. especially Acts 19:1 with 1 Corinthians 1:12; 3:5-6; etc.], an Alexandrian in reference to birth, an educated (or, "learned," NIV) man [the NASB text reads "an eloquent man"; but this translation is not very probable since the word occurs only here in the New Testament and in view of the fact that the other meaning is found several times in Greek literature outside of the Bible] came to Ephesus, being powerful in the Scriptures." His strength (i.e. another occurrence of the 'can-do,' *dynamic* word-group) was a derived "might" sourced in the divinely sufficient Scriptures. This becomes clear when the ministry of the man is observed in v. 28: "for he was powerfully (and) publicly refuting [we could paraphrase this unique doubly-compounded word 'he was flooring' or 'decking'] the Jews by showing (or, proving; or, demonstrating) by means of the Scriptures that Jesus was the Messiah." Notice that the might of Apollos' method came through the vehicle of God's persuasive words from His Word. Although he was quite apparently a very articulate and astute individual, the Bible was the real source of his evangelistic 'power-punches.'

Paul's Model

Synthesized from His Commands

Obviously, because of the heavy volume of Paul's commands bearing either explicitly or implicitly on method in ministry, the texts I have assembled represent only a small fraction of the massive data reservoir available to any investigator. Also, for the sake of processing these data, I have chosen to place them into two categories, what Paul would urge us to avoid and what he would want us to do.

What to Avoid

All kinds of warnings come into play here. For example, he warns professing Christians to look out for men who would come into their midst with manipulative methodologies. Concerning these slick-tongued heretics who were already sitting on the door-step of the church at Colossae he warns, "I am saying this [i.e. in view of the fact that all true truth and real knowledge are to be found only in Christ (Colossians 2:1-3)] that no person should deceive (or, delude) [this verb connotes 'to lead astray with side-tracking reasonings'] you with persuasive speech [i.e. with a lawyer's manipulative rhetoric so as 'to sucker' you into error]. . . . Continue to be on the lookout that no person cart you off as a captive [i.e. into heresy] by means of the philosophy which is characterized by vain deceit according to the tradition of men [i.e. bad tradition from the wrong source], according to (i.e. according to the norm or standard of; or, as measured by) the elementary principles [i.e. the 'A, B, C's'] of the world, and not according to Christ" [i.e. who is the measure and norm of true tradition] (Colossians 2:4, 8). Paul's language was vividly 'red-flagged,' because he understood the great hazard to the spiritual welfare of the Colossians. They were exceedingly vulnerable not only because of the teachings of these false teachers but also because their methods cunningly matched their malignant message. In view of this imminent danger, Paul was spiritually inoculating the Colossian believers with the wisdom of the Word (contrast the false teachers with their wisdom of the world) and his methodological 'syringe' was an earnest straight-forward presentation of the truth (contrast the false teachers with their perverse persuasions).

The Pastoral Epistles are loaded with admonitions from Paul to his young assistants. He had commissioned Timothy and Titus to assist the local churches of their respective regions so that they might become mature, God-honoring assemblies. An ever-present danger to these churches would be the threat of false teachers with their false doctrines. Sound familiar?! But, there was another danger. It was that Timothy and Titus might be tempted to do God's business men's way when dealing with such ravenous wolves. These young men could not effectively guard the flock of God by using the 'shepherding' methodologies of the world. Let me, without much commentary, simply string together a few of Paul's warnings about how Timothy and Titus were *not* to carry on God's business. Obviously, these warnings are quite applicable to those of us who today are engaged in full-time Christian service. And, furthermore, the most basic, undergirding principles of Paul's admonitions generally apply to all believers at all times.

Let me set the stage for these warnings just as Paul himself does right at the beginning of 1 Timothy:

> Just as I urged you, as I was departing into Macedonia, you should remain in Ephesus in order to command (or, direct; or give orders to) certain ones not to teach false doctrines [our term "heterodox" is derived from this Greek word-group] neither to preoccupy themselves with myths and endless genealogies, which very things bring about useless speculations rather than God's way of working, which is by faith. But the goal of the command [cf. v. 3] is love out of a cleansed (i.e. pure) heart and a good conscience and an unhypocritical faith; some, deviating, have turned aside to empty words, desiring to be law-teachers, although not understanding the things they are talking about or the things about which they confidently speak (1 Timothy 1:3-7).

These are the kinds of people Timothy would be coming up against.

With this in mind, listen to Paul's charge to Timothy at the very end of this letter. It summarizes positively what he was to do and also reinforces how he was to turn away from certain men and their methods: "O Timothy, guard the (sacred) deposit, turning away from profane, empty talk and the opposition [our word "antithesis" comes directly from this Greek term] of what is falsely called knowledge [i.e. *pseudo*-knowledge], which some people, having laid claim to it, have departed [cf. "deviating" above in 1 Timothy 1:6] in regard to the faith" (1 Timothy 6:20-21a). Timothy needed to avoid these men like the plague that they were, by *not* engaging them on their turf of vain verbiage (i.e. empty words) and pseudo-knowledge.

In 2 Timothy 2:14, 15-17a, Paul similarly writes to his young, right hand man:

> Keep reminding them of these things. Warn them before God against quarreling about words [literally, 'word-warring']; it is of no value, and only ruins [our word "catastrophe" comes from this Greek word-group] those who listen. . . . avoid godless chatter [i.e. the "profane, empty talk" also referred to in 1 Timothy 6:20], because those who indulge in it will become more and more ungodly. Their teaching will spread like gangrene (2 Timothy 2:14, 16-17a; NIV).

Now bring up alongside of these words of warning from the Apostle Paul his command and explanation at the end of chapter 2:

> Now avoid (or, reject) foolish [i.e. the 'moronic' word-group in Greek] and stupid speculations (or, arguments; or, controversies), since you know that they generate (i.e. give birth to) fights (or, quarrels; or, disputes); but a servant of the Lord must [i.e. this impersonal verb

stresses necessity] not fight (i.e. not quarrel), but rather he is to be gentle towards all, able to teach, able to bear evil without resentment, instructing with humility the ones who stand in opposition, if perhaps God might grant them repentance unto [i.e. leading them unto] a (true) knowledge of truth, and that they might come to their senses (and escape) from the trap of the devil, having been held captive by him to do that one's [i.e. the devil's] will (2 Timothy 2:23-25).

"A servant of the Lord" (v. 24) must reject humanistic ways of doing things (v. 23). Contrastingly, in attitude and activity, he must *do God's work God's way* (vs. 24-25a), and then dependently wait upon the Lord for results (vv. 25b-26). He must not pridefully engage opponents, but patiently educate them. He must not try to convince them with his tactics, but correct them in humility. Unfortunately, too many of God's 'servants' today are resorting to the methods and the means of those who oppose the truth. This negates any possibility of *doing God's business His way.*

What to Do

Having sketched out what to avoid in ministering, it is time to listen to Paul tell Timothy, Titus, and all of us what to do. Right in the middle of a 'don't-do-like-this' passage (cf. 2 Timothy 2:14, 16-17a above), he wrote: "Take pains to present yourself approved [i.e. 'tested and true'] to God (as) an unashamed laborer, one who correctly cuts [cf. the Greek translation of the Old Testament for this term in Proverbs 3:6 and 11:5] the word of the Truth" [i.e. one who correctly handles and accurately conveys the word of truth] (2 Timothy 2:15). What Paul generalizes in 2 Timothy 2:15, he fleshes out in more detail in chapter 4, v. 2: "Herald (i.e. proclaim) the Word;

stand by (i.e. be ready) in season, out of season [i.e. when it is convenient and when it is inconvenient]; correct (or, reprove) [i.e. through an accurate handling and a straightforward presentation of the words from the Word, God's mouth-pieces are able to fulfill such specific ministries as this one (cf. the same word-group used for the 'reproof' in connection with the "conviction" of the Holy Spirit in John 16:8, and for the "reproof" of the Scriptures in 2 Timothy 3:16) and those which follow as examples], rebuke, exhort (or, encourage) [this word is related to the Holy Spirit's primary designation in John 14-16, i.e. the *Paraclete*], with all long-suffering [i.e. normally *patience* relating to people] and doctrine" [cf. the NIV's "careful instruction"]. This is the way Timothy was and we are to *do God's business.*

By the way, if we do honor God in this fashion, don't expect the applause of *professing* Christendom. Nevertheless, we must 'hang in there' if we ever hope to be divinely recognized as faithful servants (cf. 1 Corinthians 4:1-5). Consequently, Paul continues like this in vv. 3-5 of 2 Timothy 4:

> For the time will come [I'm not 'into' identifying prophecy-fulfillments, but just meditate on the current status of Christianity!] when men will not put up with sound doctrine. Instead, to suit their own desires, they will gather around them a great number of teachers to say what their itching ears want to hear. They will turn their ears away from the truth and turn aside to myths. But you, keep your head in all situations, endure hardship, do the work of an evangelist, discharge all the duties of your ministry (NIV).

We dare not give people what they want, but must give them what they need, and what they need is clearly spelled out in God's Word.

I want to round out this particular discussion with a verse from Titus. In the first paragraph of the body of the apostle's epistle to him, Paul reminds Titus why he had left him behind in Crete, namely, to assist the churches in the various cities so that they might become solid and strong (cf. Titus 1:5). A primary way through which Titus was to do this was by recognizing and appointing elders in those churches. And, quite obviously, such men must be qualified biblically (i.e. vv. 6-9). They must be men of integrity (vv. 6-8) who are anchored in the Bible so that they can protect God's flock (v. 9). Each of these men characteristically must be "clinging to the faithful word which is according to the teaching [literally, "the according to the doctrine trustworthy Word"], in order that he may be able [i.e. the *dynamic* word-group returns; and, once again, the elder's 'power' and 'can do' comes from the Word] both to exhort (or, to encourage) [as noted above in 2 Timothy 4:2 this word is from the *Paraclete* word group] with (or, in) healthy (or, sound) teaching (or, doctrine) and to refute [i.e. the 'reproof' word-group also returns; again, cf. John 16:8; 2 Timothy 3:16; 4:2; etc.] the ones who are speaking against (it)" (Titus 1:9). The church's leaders must be men of the Word who faithfully unleash its power in order to protect and preserve the flock of God.

Summarized in His Testimony

Paul's personal model for ministry is contained in 1 Corinthians 2:1-5. This little paragraph, crouched in the context of the apostle's commission and in the setting of the hostilities of the world, is a methodological gem stone. No other passage reveals as much about *doing God's business God's way* as this one does. It is my prayer that we all will make Paul's testimony our own throughout life-times of ministry.

The most important feature of the total context of 1 Corinthians is the war between two wisdoms, the wisdom of the world, a pseudo-wisdom, and the wisdom of

God, the only true wisdom. All the sad symptoms of im-maturity that Paul dealt with in this epistle are attribut-able to the fact that many of these professing people of Christ at Corinth were enamored with worldly wisdom. This natural tendency in men was all the more catalyzed by their Greek culture. Even after the so-called "Golden Era" of Greek history, those of that ethnic heritage re-garded themselves as the cream of the crop in reference to intelligence and culture. We saw indications of this phenomenon when I briefly commented on Acts 17:16ff. And remember, right after Paul left Athens, he went to Corinth (Acts 18:1) where he encountered more of the same kind of intellectual arrogance. He would have had no trouble identifying the Corinthians' arrogantly auton-omous world-and-life view. It would manifest itself quickly. Quite obviously, when Paul arrived and preached the Gospel of God's sovereign grace, antitheti-cal world-and-life views along with their respective "wis-doms" collided. Also, quite obviously, no matter where Paul went, he knew theologically that this would be the case. However, after having been through the 'grinder' in Athens (not to mention the hounding Jewish antagonists before that, in town after town; cf. Acts 17:1-15), he need-ed to re-commit himself to his decision *to do God's busi-ness God's way*. And Paul informed the Corinthians in 1 Corinthians 2:1-5 that he had done just that when he came to minister the Gospel to them; the stakes were eternally too high to do otherwise.

In 1 Corinthians 2:1-5 we are going to find four per-sonal disclosures by Paul which crystallize the biblical pattern for *doing God's business God's way*. Verse one con-tains a follow-up disclosure regarding his commission. He candidly confessed to them: "And when I came to you, brothers, I did not come with [literally, 'according to, as measured by the norm of,' etc.; in this case the "norm" would have been the rhetoric and reasonings of the orators and debaters that they were used to hearing] excellence (or, preeminence; or, superiority) of word or of wisdom, as I was proclaiming (or, announcing; or declaring; i.e. publicly preaching) to you the mystery [a textual variant reads "witness"; either term can be used for the Gospel message] of God." Interestingly, Paul began with a negative affirmation most likely due to the cultural background of these Greeks. When he entered town and began to minister, he objectively and emphatically denied that he had operated according to the oratorical precedent of the Greek 'hot shots.' Every word in this verse's most crucial prepositional phrase would have been a buzz-word to these people. Yet, Paul says that there is no sense in which he came in among them with 'that which rises above in reference to rhetoric or reason,' with 'superiority of eloquence or of persuasive arguments,' with 'preeminence of fancy words or of exhibitions of intellect,' etc. Why was he so utterly resistant to giving them what they were used to and wanted to hear?

Well, if you remember, I labeled this first-disclosure "a follow-up disclosure." That is because it follows up a revelation about Paul's commission recorded in chapter 1. First Corinthians 1:17 contains yet more insight into Paul's Damascus Road experience of Acts 9. When Christ commissioned Paul into the Gospel ministry, our Lord carefully spelled out how he was to carry on God's business along with how he was *not* to share and to serve. Paul testifies: "For Christ did not send me [i.e. a commissioned sending] to (continually) baptize, but [i.e. a strong contrasting conjunction] to keep on preaching the Gospel [i.e. to keep on announcing and proclaiming the Good News], not [i.e. 'He, Christ, did _not_ commission and send me to do this in this manner'] with wisdom of word, in order that the cross of Christ might not be made void" (or, "be emptied of its power," NIV). Very interestingly, the phrase that I translated literally as "with wisdom of word" here contains the same two nouns, but in reverse order, as found in 1 Corinthians 2:1 (i.e. "excellence *of word* or *of wisdom*"). No matter their order or how these two terms were linked together, they stood for the philosophical style which for so long had characterized the communications of the Greek orators and debaters. So, Christ had commanded Paul at his commissioning that he must never carry on the work of the Gospel by such means and methods.

Furthermore, Paul's task as defined by the Lord Himself was to preach (i.e. announce) the Good News. The announcing of Good News would never allow for any kind of dialoguing or debating. 'News-casters' are supposed to report the facts accurately and plainly, and the *Good-News* facts are not to be opened up to the forums and editorializings of men. Therefore, Paul, knowing the Lord would be constantly looking on and evaluating his ministry, came to the Corinthians (and to all the other people in various cities) "publicly proclaiming" the Gospel (1 Corinthians 2:1). His ministry of preaching allowed absolutely no room for dialoguing and debating with people whose 'thought-formulations of the heart were exclusively and continually evil' (Genesis 6:5), 'who were by nature dead in their trespasses and sins' (Ephesians 2:1, 3), who 'were enemies in their minds' (Colossians 1:21), 'who would not openly receive the things of the Spirit' (1 Corinthians 2:14 in context), etc. He had to and wanted *to do Christ's business* (1 Corinthians 2:1) *Christ's way* (1 Corinthians 1:17).

Now if anyone should be doubting whether these Pauline principles pertain to us because he had been commissioned *as an apostle*, I would urge that you contemplate the nature of the Great Commission. Matthew 28:19-20 contains Christ's Gospel marching orders for us. We certainly are not apostles; a foundation is only laid once (Ephesians 2:20). However, our message is the same; it has not changed. Also, the nature of the people to whom Christ sends us has not changed; they're still just as resistant as the Corinthians were. Therefore, our method should be identical to Paul's.

Now, let's move on to 1 Corinthians 2:2 wherein Paul makes an undaunted disclosure concerning his subject matter, saying: "For I determined to know nothing among you except Jesus Christ and Him crucified" (1 Corinthians 2:2, NASB). Paul had come to this decision undoubtedly heavily influenced by his Lord's commission of him. His decision concerning content could also be rendered: 'I judged fit,' 'I made it my business,' "I resolved" (NIV), etc. He had to make up his mind about sticking to the content of the Gospel even when it seemed so offensive to people. The same decision is demanded of modern ministers of the Gospel, be they 'lay' people or 'vocational' people.

Let's keep on tracking with Paul and observe his discrimination involving what his content would be. He first tells us what he eliminated; he had made up his mind "to know nothing" among these Corinthians. What's that supposed to mean? Well, he is drawing upon another buzz-word of the hot-shot philosophers of that day. Many of them in an attempt to capture the attention of an audience would bait them by saying, "I know something." Then they would begin to unpack their supposedly brilliant philosophical tid-bits. This practice may have been, at least partially, intimated in Luke's parenthetical observation found back in Acts 17:21. So the statement "I know something" was a code clause for one claiming to be a philosopher. Now, catch the force of Paul's deliberate denial when he came to the Corinthians who had been constantly exposed to such arrogant claims: I made a firm decision "to know nothing among you." In one fell swoop, he junked man's way of doing business, refusing, even with a ten-foot pole, to touch man's knowledge and worldly '"wisdom."'

Does this mean he had nothing to say to the Corinthians. On the contrary, the "except" that follows introduces what he elevated. With this little word he draws a line around his exclusive subject matter. And the content of his communications was the Gospel message with its twin focuses on the Person of the Savior and the provision of the Savior. His exclusive subject matter of the Person and work of Christ would have included all the data of Christology and Soteriology. The more instruction in these most vital areas the better! By referring to our Lord as "Jesus Christ," he undoubtedly had carefully explained to them that this Jesus was both Savior (cf., e.g., the 'Hebrew lesson' about the theological significance of the name "Jesus" in Matthew 1:21) and Christ (i.e. Messiah).

So far so good. After all, it was not the name "Jesus" that stirred up the 'intelligencia' at Athens (cf. Acts 17, again). However, Paul's content by commissioned necessity also had to include the crucifixion and the resurrection. Modern methodologists would undoubtedly balk now. Some of them might even secretly contemplate that he was an awfully slow learner. I can hear them mumbling under their breath:

> Don't you know, Paul, that you should adjust your message, at least at the outset, to the cultural climate of the hearers? Don't you understand that you cannot spring something on people which is known to be offensive to them? Don't you remember how most 'learned' Greeks sneer at any mentioning of the resurrection of the dead? Luke even noted this in Acts 17:32! Furthermore, you yourself just said that "the word of the cross is foolishness" [i.e. moronic or silly stuff] and that a crucified Christ [i.e. Messiah] is, "on the one hand, a stumbling block [i.e. an offense] to Jews, and on the other hand foolishness to Gentiles" [i.e. especially to "Greeks," v. 22] (1 Corinthians 1:18a; 23b)!

And so goes the thinking of methodological compromisers. By the way, they are particularly good at excerpting pieces of Scripture and/or taking statements out of context. For example, as Luke went on to note in Acts 17, although some did sneer at the mentioning of a crucified and resurrected Messiah, "a few men became followers of Paul [i.e. as disciples to learn more about Christ] and believed. Among them was Dionysius, a member of the Areopagus, also a woman named Damaris, and a number of others" (v. 34). Also, the greater context of Paul's cultural 'concessions' of 1 Corinthians 1:18a and 23b brings them into proper focus:

> For the word, that is the word about the cross, is indeed, on the one hand, foolishness [i.e. '*moronic*'] in reference to the ones who are perishing, but, on the other hand, it [i.e. the Gospel of the cross] is the power [i.e. the '*dynamic*' 'can-do'] of God in reference to the ones who are being saved; for it still stands written, "I [i.e. God] will destroy the wisdom of the wise ones [i.e. the pseudo-wisdom of the pseudo-wise] and the intelligence (or, understanding; or, comprehension, etc.) of the intelligent ones [i.e. the psuedo-intelligence of the pseudo 'intellegensia'] I will confound (or, [fatally] frustrate it)." Where is a wise person? Where is a scribe [cf. the NIV's "scholar"]? Where is a disputer (or, debater) of this age? Has not God shown to be foolish [i.e. '*moronic*'] the wisdom [i.e. pseudo-wisdom] of the world?! For since in the wisdom of God the world did not know God by means of its own wisdom, God was well pleased by means of the foolishness of the proclaimed message to save (or, deliver; or, rescue) the ones who are believing. Jews [leaving out the "because" conjunction in view of Paul's forthcoming punch-line in v. 23] (customarily) ask for sign-miracles and [literally this verse contains a "both . . . and" association of Jews and Gentiles; however, in view of their respective preferences, it makes the combination too hard to render into English—the emphasis of

the "both/and" structure may be to indicate
the universal condemnation of both major
classes of humanity; cf. Romans 1:18-3:20
again] Greeks (habitually) seek wisdom, but
we are preaching [i.e. the 'hearlding' verb of 2
Timothy 4:2] Christ crucified, on the one hand,
a stumbling block to Jews, and on the other
hand, foolishness [i.e. *'moronic'* stuff] to the
Gentiles; however, to those who are the called
ones, both to Jews and to Greeks, Christ [i.e.
Messiah] the power [i.e. that *'dynamic'* efficient
saving power] of God and the wisdom of God,
because the foolishness of God is wiser than
men and the weakness of God is stronger than
men (1 Corinthians 1:18-25).

Yes, the Gospel is offensive. Yes, it was offensive to
those Greeks who wanted nothing to do with a crucified
Christ. But in that Gospel of "Jesus Christ and Him crucified" is man's only hope for a deliverance that endures
into eternity. In view of this non-negotiable biblical truth,
how could Paul compromise on content? How can we??

Verse 3 of 1 Corinthians 2 should be comforting to all
of us. Sometimes Paul is painted as a fearless 'maniac' in
ministry. That caricature is far from a correct picture of
the apostle. He was bold but not brazen. He, better than
anyone else, knew that he had feet of clay; he more than
anyone else except his Lord, understood how dependent
he was. Consequently, in v. 3 he helps us to see what was
going on inside of him by giving us this transparent disclosure about his own dependence. The mightiest of mis-
sionaries operated according to a personal declaration of
dependence. He too, as an impotent spiritual medic was
totally reliant upon God and His sufficient resources.
Here's his brief but revealing testimony: "And in weakness [the 'without strength' word-group] and in fear and
with much trembling, I came to you" (1 Corinthians 2:3).
Was this just because of his challenging experiences of re-

cent months [i.e. Acts 17]? Maybe partially, but it was more than that. Predominately, it was because he well understood 'the guts and the glory' of Christian ministry. As a matter of fact, in his second preserved letter to these same people, he talked about it extensively (cf. 2 Corinthians 2:14-6:10). Listen to how Paul launches that high flight on Christian ministry:

> But thanks be to God, who always leads us in His triumph in Christ, and manifests through us [i.e. through us, His mouth-piece channels] the sweet aroma of the knowledge of Him in every place. [Wow, what a glorious ministry! Many may want to enlist immediately into full-time service. Great, but keep on reading.] For we are a fragrance of Christ to God among those who are being saved and among those who are perishing [there is glory, but there is also the 'guts' reality when it comes to ministering the Gospel]; to the one an aroma from death to death, to the other an aroma from life to life (2 Corinthians 2:14-16a; NASB).

In view of this awesome synopsis of the Gospel ministry, Paul cries out representationally, "And who is equal [or, adequate; or sufficient for] to such a task?" This rhetorical question is to be answered, "No mere man!" Certainly, Paul, in the presence of such a high and holy calling, regarded himself as being thoroughly and totally insufficient. But he goes on, in chapter 3, to revel in God's sufficiencies: "Not that we are adequate in ourselves to consider anything as *coming* from ourselves, but our adequacy is from God" [i.e. the source of our sufficiency is in Him] (2 Corinthians 3:5; NASB). As long as we're talking about Paul's declarations of dependence, remember how he contrasted his own insufficiency with God's power-provisions in 2 Corinthians 10:3-5. We, like Paul, must understand that we are absolutely bankrupt of spiritual power, in and of ourselves. We carry on our ministries for the Lord while we are "in flesh" [i.e. in our finite, feeble, and frail condition]; however, not "according to the flesh" [i.e. not as powered by our own resources]. Therefore, we must dependently appropriate and apply the powerful provisions of God so that we can do *His work His way.*

Returning to 1 Corinthians 2, Paul's fourth and final disclosure comes straight at us in vv. 4-5. It is a 'wide-angled' disclosure about his method. In verse 4, he stresses the impact of that method, and then in the purpose clause of verse 5, he deals with the importance of it. Verse 4 really summarizes both verses 1 and 2. To make his point, Paul uses a stark contrast pertaining to people's power. In the first part of this 'not this, but that' contrast, Paul again emphatically denies that his method was like that of the philosophers, orators, and debaters that the Corinthians were so familiar with. His method was not like theirs in content nor in communication: "And my speech [literally, word] and my message [i.e. the same term as the "preached *message*" of 1:21] were not with persuasive words of wisdom [cf. the "wisdom of word" in 1:17, and the combination of "word and wisdom" in 2:1; i.e. not according to the methods of the pagan philosophers], . . ." (1 Corinthians 2:4a). Besides employing the two words that he has been using all along to expose such rhetorical manipulators, he adds a new qualifier *"persuasive* words of wisdom." This term was also a buzz word that was frequently applied to a lawyer's persuasion. It is conceptually related to a term I already called to your attention in Colossians 2:4 (i.e. don't let anyone 'reason you off-course by *persuasive* speech').

Now in contrast with their methods which he stoutly rejected, he goes on to summarize the impact of his own method, a method that was confirmed by the potency of God: "but [i.e. the strongest contrasting conjunction] my speech and the message I proclaimed were (or came [i.e. to you]) in demonstration (or, the proof) of the Spirit and of power" (v. 4b). Here "proof" stands opposed to the razzle dazzle rhetoric (i.e. "the persuasive words") of the oratorical hot shots, and "of the Spirit and power" contrasts with "of (worldly) wisdom." Ironically, in spite of all the razzmatazz, their method was utterly impotent as to delivering people from their bondage, while Paul's was the vehicle for the sufficiencies of God. The apostle had humbly and dependently appropriated the divine resources of the Spirit and His Word (review chapter 6, "The Sufficiencies of God for Service"). Remember the "proof" or "demonstration" of the Spirit working with His Sword, for example, in 1 Thessalonians 1:5 and 2:13.

Now, if this disclosure seemed to the Corinthians to be nothing more than methodological theory, Paul was determined to wake them up with his purpose clause of v. 5. He did *God's business God's way* because *their* eternal welfare was at stake: "in order that your faith might not be in [i.e. rest on] the wisdom of men, but [i.e. the same strong contrasting conjunction Paul used in the previous contrast of v. 4] in [i.e. rest on] the power [i.e. the omnipotent '*dynamic*'] of God." You see, if Paul had ministered to them man's way, the Corinthians' trust would have rested on a foundation that was sure to crumble. However, because he was faithful to his commission, their trust was grounded on the foundation which will never fail, the power of God.

So Paul was a faithful servant throughout his ministry; no one doubts that. But, the real question is "Will you be also?" Are you willing, by the grace and enablements of our Lord, *to do God's business God's way*? Or, are you willing to risk evacuating the cross of its life-saving and life-sustaining power?

Chapter 8
Some Suggested
Models For Ministring

No matter what kind of Christian ministry we may be involved in, the cardinal prerequisite is that we constantly keep in mind every facet of the doctrines of sovereign grace. Without these biblical truths as our pilot, we will stray off course. So, building upon that theological foundation, let me suggest a few 'how to's.' I'll divide my practical suggestions into two broad categories of application, those that pertain to ministering to lost people and those that pertain to tending for the professing flock of God.

Sharing the Gospel

Sharing the Good News with a desperate, dying world of lost people is every Christian's responsibility. As we go about doing our share in the carrying out of the Great Commission, we need to remember God's infallible diagnosis of the natural man's heart. Being sold out to self, sin and Satan, the unsaved person is not objective nor open-minded when exposed to the issues of eternity. He has a vested interest in protecting his alleged autonomy; therefore, he will resist spiritual things with every ounce of his rebellious being. Smooth talk and 'brilliant arguments' on our part will, at best, be ineffectual and, at worse, prove tragically counterproductive. Often such methods pour gasoline on his flames of burning rejection.

Therefore, we must constantly acknowledge that God's sufficiencies alone can rescue him. These are the divinely powerful weapons of the Word and the Spirit. Concerning the Word of God, whether in hand or in heart at the time, try to assess if the person has any kind of 're-ligious background.' This sometimes is a hindrance, but it could help in certain cases to determine at what level you may communicate biblical truth to him. For those from a pure pagan background, you may have to communicate wisely summarizing key biblical truths like Paul did in Acts 17:16ff. Wherever possible try to quote or paraphrase the passages that contribute to an outline presentation of the essentials of the Gospel. I still prefer personal adaptations of the old "Romans' road." After all, that epistle is really a 'Gospel tract' which moves from and through the doctrine of sin to the Good News of grace and faith. When quoting or paraphrasing use a formula something like "God says," or "the Bible says," or "God says in the Bible." To the pure pagan, saying, "John says" or "Paul writes," etc. could leave the impression that these are no more than some guys who go to your church!

Also, quite frequently, some so-called 'witnesses' try to prove the Bible before they use the Bible. Others get side-tracked when they are challenged by the pagan, then they try to defend it logically with so-called evidences. How blasphemously ironic! Who do we think that we are when we are pridefully pulled into doing this? It's God's Word! It is attested to by no man, but only by the sovereign Spirit who wrote it and who powerfully breathes through every word of it.

Consequently, in every witnessing context, we need to firmly and lovingly persevere in a scriptural presentation of the Gospel. Every "Where did Cain get his wife?" and "What about this or what about that?" needs to be 'tabled' when dealing with crafty-hearted people with an atheistic world-and-life view. This *humanly* impossible task of communicating with them as clearly as possible on a two-dimensional plane without getting in the way of the Gospel should drive us to unceasing prayer, prayer for ourselves that the Lord might suppress our pride of performance, and then prayer for the one who stands in desperate need of rescue from sin's bondage. We need always to pray that the Spirit would use the words from His Word coming forth faithfully from of our mouths to accomplish His sovereign pleasure in that person's life.

Serving the Saints

The same basic method needs to be followed when ministering unto professing believers because of their man-centered hangovers. When serving the flock, we exercise our scriptural obligations most faithfully when we draw our dynamic data from the Word and present those truths caringly in a straight-forward manner humbly submitting ourselves and the results to the sovereign Spirit.

Counseling

The body of Christ is to be the ultimate corporate context 'for iron sharpening iron.' After Paul prayed for the blessings and power of God to fill the Body of Christ at Rome (Romans 15:13), he said this about them: "I myself am convinced, my brothers, that you yourselves are full of goodness, complete in knowledge and competent to instruct one another" (Romans 15:14; NIV). Although not operating infallibly like the Word of God and the Spirit of God, the people of God, in a very real sense, are a third means of grace. By relying on those *primary* means of grace, the members of the Body are able "to instruct, admonish, warn, encourage," etc. [the compound Greek word basically connotes 'to influence the mind of'] one another for the good and growth of the Body. Paul summarized his own ministry to the Body like this in Colossians 1:28: "Whom [i.e. referring back to Christ of whom he has so wondrously spoken in vv. 15ff.] we are proclaiming, instructing (or warning; or, admonishing, etc.; the same key activity mentioned in Romans 15:14) every man and teaching every man with all wisdom [i.e. with God's wisdom], in order that we might present every man mature [i.e. the *ultimate* goal is perfection] in Christ." He also expected the Colossian believers (and us) to be about this task of mutual ministry: "Let the Word of Christ be at home in [and among] you richly (i.e. abundantly), with all wisdom [i.e. again, biblical wisdom] teaching and instructing [i.e. again that Romans 15:14 applicationally multifaceted activity] one another . . ." (Colossians 3:16a).

These activities of which Paul speaks often take the form of what we call counseling today. Unfortunately, although there are many people out there claiming to do 'biblical counseling,' their methods do not indicate that the Word of God is dwelling in them deeply and richly. Just as philosophy has no place in preaching (1 Corinthians 2:1-5), the secular influences of psychology have no place in counseling. On the other hand, this does not mean that we are simply to carry around a small box of assorted verses like biblical Band-Aids slapping them on various 'wounds.'

What "the Word of God being at home in us richly" does mean is that we do have a full assortment of biblical Band-Aids and that we use them directly when particular sins or patterns of sin call for a given 'specific dressing.' But there are times when no verse or passage neatly covers the wound. In these situations "the Word of God dwelling in us richly" calls for a theological richness, a deep reservoir of biblical wisdom. Indeed, such wisdom comes from a deep and broad knowledge of the Scriptures, but more than that, it is divinely dispensed to those who pray for it. They must also pray for themselves that they not glory in themselves when God is pleased to allow it to flow through them. And, needless to say, they need to pray earnestly that God's Word which is synthesized into this wisdom would move powerfully in the heart of a wounded sheep.

You who are pastors in full-time service are aware of the fact that for the aforementioned reasons counseling is usually more difficult than preaching or teaching. However, if you carefully listen to people with your *biblical* (i.e. with your physical and *theological*) ears open, you have an advantage in counseling situations. If you're prone to making a lot of applications throughout your messages from the pulpit, you're usually shooting from the hip at a conjectured target. (That's why I prefer to let the Spirit make His own applications from the *texts* of my messages; after all, He doesn't shoot from the hip, but accurately hits multiple targets with His sawed-off, applicational shot gun!) Now, returning to the advantage of the counseling session, because of an intimacy stemming from longer periods of personal dialogues leading to deeper disclosures of a given person's 'problem,' accurate applications often manifest themselves as spiritual 'no brainers.' In that intimate context, it is quite likely that we, dependent upon all the previous divine resources mentioned above, will be able to identify, expose, challenge, and help to correct the person's wrong thinking and behavior.

Teaching and Preaching

Before I talk directly about applicational suggestions for teaching and preaching, I need to stress the significance of both sin and the sufficiencies of God one more time. Never underestimate the flock's (nor your own) problem of sin hangover. Because of this reality, the dynamics *of God* are still demanded in order to mature and to correct the sheep. Therefore, when we are functioning as teachers and/or preachers, we have one basic responsibility: "Preach the Word!" (2 Timothy 4:2). Please note the simple, yet profound, significance of this command's syntax: "(You) *preach* (i.e. herald; or proclaim) *the Word!*" The content of our preaching must therefore be the Word and nothing but the Word. We must not simply preach about it or spring-board from it; we must clearly expound all the facets of every text's contents. Consequently, *genuine* textual exposition is the only acceptable means to that end.

Now, true textual exposition is more than word studies. 'You believe in verbal, plenary inspiration; you do well!' But we must understand that not just the words of the Bible are God-breathed, but so also are the relationships of those words to one another. Without syntax, there would be no sense. So, if the relationships of the words of a phrase, the words of phrases to respective clauses, the respective clauses to units of thought, the units of thought to main sectional burdens, etc. are the divine product of the Spirit of God, and they are, a full description of all these essential elements is essential to unleash the full instruction and impact of every biblical text. We must take apart and put back together all the pieces of a passage so that when it is communicated, it will come forth "not *as* the word of men, but *for* what it really is, the Word of God, which also effectually performs its work in you who believe" (1 Thessalonians 2:13b; NASB).

Admittedly, this involves a lot of hard work (cf., e.g., 1 Timothy 5:17b), but no short-cuts in preparation are allowed if we are going *to do God's business God's way.* "Handling accurately the Word of truth" (2 Timothy 2:15) is a heavy-duty responsibility, but it is also a sacred privilege. You see, if we've done our hard homework and accurately and clearly communicate the words and syntax of a passage, then the Spirit of God once again speaks to the people of God.

Needless to say, throughout the whole sermonic process, from preparation to presentation, we need to be praying earnestly for divine enablement and also that the sovereign Spirit would use the words from His Word to change hearts, beginning with our own.

Now, for a few suggestions on how to do what I've been talking about. Rather than trying to explain the method, please permit me to exemplify it. What follows are a few selected samples. I have deliberately chosen some texts that I have previously discussed, either briefly or more thoroughly. Consequently, to see how some meat might be hung on these structural skeletons, consult those former discussions.

The place to begin is with a diagram of the text. A diagram is a picture of the passage's syntax. It keeps us honest. Our outlines must come from this structural map. They must be true to the text at every structural level. Furthermore, they need to be as descriptive as possible in their reflection of the larger (i.e. these units will be the main points) and smaller (i.e. these units will be the subpoints, *et. al*) syntactical parts of the text. In this way we let our text do the outlining of itself. A heading-synopsis should precede your outline. It should synthesize the major burden of that text stating how many main points are forthcoming and how they develop the text's major message. This introductory synopsis is usually called a plural-noun propositional statement.

Please accept the following illustrative samples not as the last organizational words on these passages but as suggested basic models for consideration and evaluation. For those unfamiliar with Hebrew and Greek, I have suspended English translations over the various words and phrases.

EXAMPLE #1
A SUGGESTED DIAGRAM AND
OUTLINE OF GENESIS 6:5

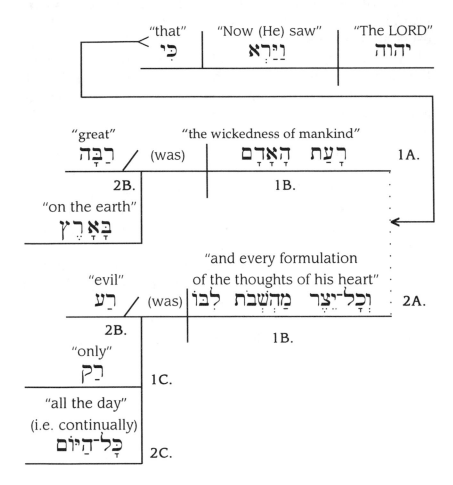

Genesis 6:5 contains two Divine Insights into the dark reality of human depravity.

    1A. The first divine insight exposes the breadth of depravity.
        1B. The disease
        2B. The epidemic
    2A. The second divine insight exposes the depth of depravity.
        1B. The seedbed
        2B. The severity:
            1C. Confirmed by its hold.
            2C. Confirmed by its habit.

EXAMPLE #2
DIAGRAM AND OUTLINE OF PSALM 19:7-8

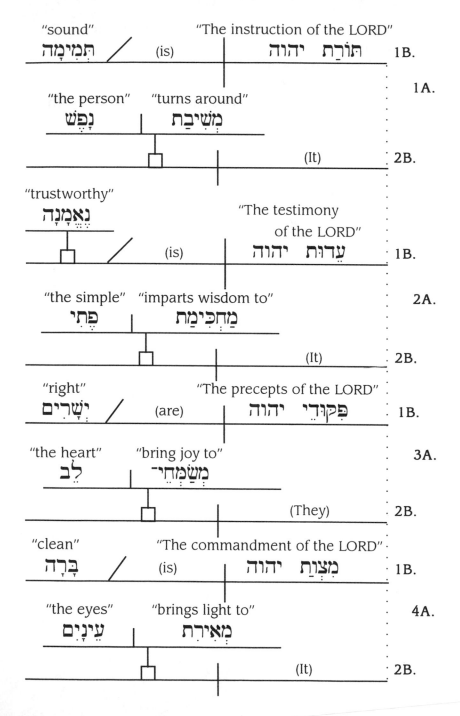

"sound" / "The instruction of the LORD"
תְּמִימָה / (is) | תּוֹרַת יהוה 1B.

                                                    1A.

"the person" "turns around"
נֶפֶשׁ | מְשִׁיבַת

                                  (It) 2B.

"trustworthy"
נֶאֱמָנָה   "The testimony
                      of the LORD"
                   (is) | עֵדוּת יהוה 1B.

"the simple" "imparts wisdom to"   2A.
פֶּתִי | מַחְכִּימַת

                                  (It) 2B.

"right" "The precepts of the LORD"
יְשָׁרִים / (are) | פִּקּוּדֵי יהוה 1B.

"the heart" "bring joy to"   3A.
לֵב | מְשַׂמְּחֵי־

                                  (They) 2B.

"clean" "The commandment of the LORD"
בָּרָה / (is) | מִצְוַת יהוה 1B.

"the eyes" "brings light to"   4A.
עֵינָיִם | מְאִירַת

                                  (It) 2B.

After having painted a poetic picture of the revelation of God in nature (vv. 1-6), "the sweet psalmist of Israel" praises the LORD for His special revelation in the Bible, launching out with four couplets of confidence in the sufficiency of God's Word.

1A. (v. 7a) In his first couplet of confidence, he focuses on the sound Word and its changing power.
   1B. He identifies what the Word of God *is* by:
      1C. its designation: "the direction of the LORD"
      2C. its description: it is "perfect"
   2B. He gives thanks for what the Word of God *does* because of:
      1C. its dynamic: it 'turns around'
      2C. its direction: a "person"

2A. (v. 7b) In his second couplet of confidence, he focuses on the faithful Word and its maturing power.
   1B. He identifies what the Word of God *is* by:
      1C. its designation: "the testimony of the LORD"
      2C. its description: it is "trustworthy"
   2B. He gives thanks for what the Word of God *does* because of:
      1C. its dynamic: it "imparts wisdom"
      2C. its direction: to "the simple"

3A. (v. 8a) In his third couplet of confidence, he focuses on the ethical Word and its encouraging power.
   1B. He identifies what the Word of God *is* by:
      1C. its designation: "the precepts of the LORD"
      2C. its description: they are ethically 'level and straight'
   2B. He gives thanks for what the Word of God *does* because of:

           1C. its dynamic: it 'brings joy'

           2C. its direction: to the "heart"

4A. (v. 8b) In his fourth couplet of confidence, he focuses on the pure Word and its illuminating power.

    1B. He identifies what the Word of God *is* by:

        1C. its designation: "the commandment of the LORD"

        2C. its description: it is spiritually "clean"

    2B. He gives thanks for what the Word of God *does* because of:

        1C. its dynamic: it "brings light to"

        2C. its direction: to the "eyes" of the heart

EXAMPLE #3
DIAGRAM AND OUTLINE OF
1 CORINTHIANS 2:14

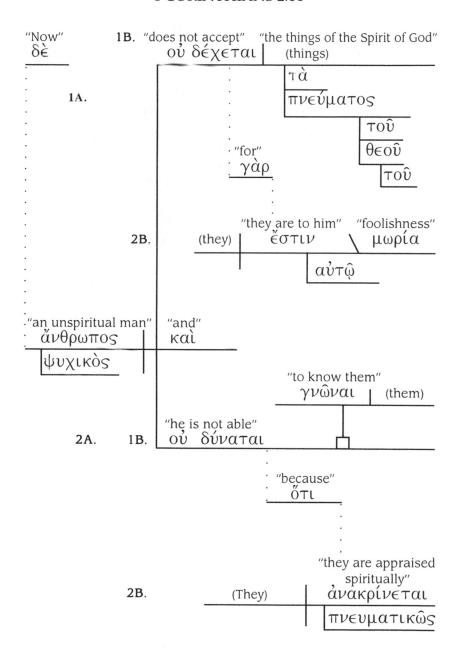

In 1 Corinthians 2:14 two spiritually fatal complications show how utterly helpless and hopeless an unregenerate person is.

1A. (v. 14a) His first fatal complication is his inhospitability to the Gospel.
   1B. This inhospitability is exposed: 'The unregenerate person refuses to put out his welcome mat for spiritual things.'
   2B. This inhospitability is explained: 'as far as the unregenerate person is concerned, spiritual things are silly.'
2A. (v. 14b) His second fatal complication is his inability to grasp the Gospel.
   1B. This inability is exposed: 'The unregenerate person has absolutely no capacity to understand spiritual things.'
   2B. This inability is explained: 'The unregenerate person lacks the spiritual equipment to process spiritual things.'

EXAMPLE #4
DIAGRAM AND OUTLINE OF
1 CORINTHIANS 2:1-5

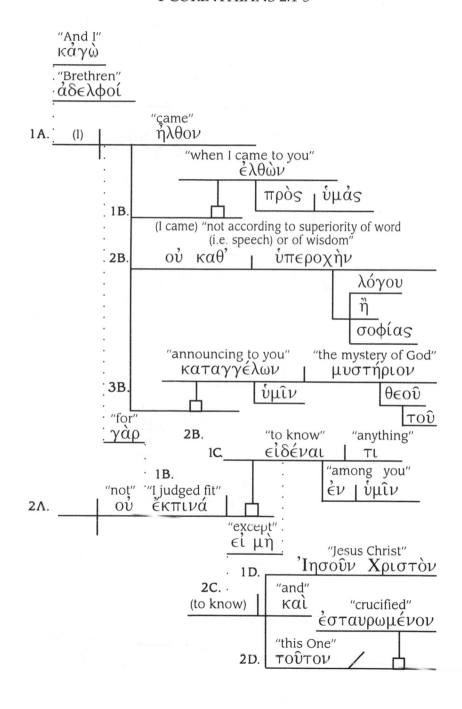

EXAMPLE #4 con't

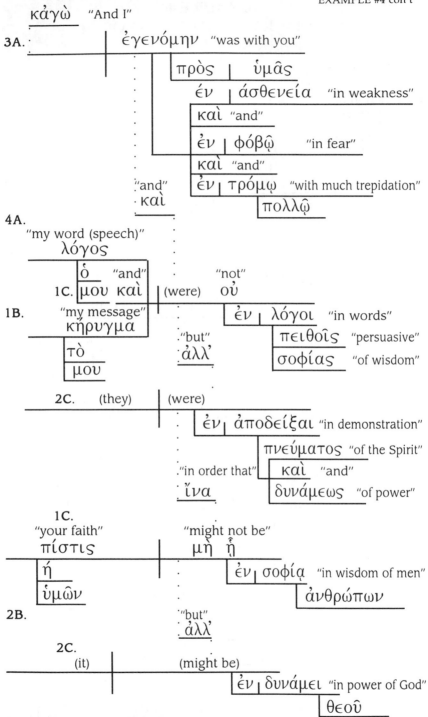

κἀγὼ "And I"

3A. ἐγενόμην "was with you"

πρὸς | ὑμᾶς

ἐν | ἀσθενείᾳ "in weakness"

καὶ "and"

ἐν | φόβῳ "in fear"

καὶ "and"

"and" ἐν | τρόμῳ "with much trepidation"

καὶ πολλῷ

4A.

"my word (speech)"
λόγος

ὁ "and" "not"

1C. μου καὶ (were) οὐ

1B. "my message"
κήρυγμα ἐν | λόγοι "in words"

πειθοῖς "persuasive"

τὸ "but" σοφίας "of wisdom"

μου ἀλλ'

2C. (they) (were)

ἐν | ἀποδείξαι "in demonstration"

πνεύματος "of the Spirit"

"in order that" καὶ "and"

ἵνα δυνάμεως "of power"

1C.
"your faith" "might not be"
πίστις μὴ ᾖ

ἡ ἐν | σοφίᾳ "in wisdom of men"

ὑμῶν ἀνθρώπων

2B. "but"
ἀλλ'

2C.
(it) (might be)

ἐν | δυνάμει "in power of God"

θεοῦ

In this passage four personal disclosures by Paul reflect the biblical pattern for *doing God's business God's way.*

1A. Verse 1 contains Paul's follow-up disclosure regarding his commission (cf. 1:17).
    1B. *The fact that he came* ties back into his commission.
    2B. *How he did not come* ties back into his commission: not with human tatics
    3B. *How he did come* ties back into his commission: with a divine proclamation
2A. Verse 2 contains Paul's undaunted disclosure concerning his content (or subject matter).
    1B. His decision relating to his content.
    2B. His discrimination relating to his content.
        1C. What he eliminated: human philosophies
        2C. What he elevated:
            1D. The Person of the Savior
            2D. The provision of the Savior
3A. Verse 3 contains Paul's candid disclosure about his dependence: he was inadequate for Gospel ministry.
4A. Verses 4-5 contain Paul's panoramic disclosure regarding his method of ministry.
    1B. (v. 4) The impact of this method:
        1C. His method was not that which was common to mere men.
        2C. His method was that which was confirmed by God.
    2B (v. 5) The importance of this method.
        1C. His method did not leave the trust of precious people grounded on a finite foundation which would crumble.
        2C. His method led to the trust of precious people being grounded on an infinite foundation which would never crack.

Scripture Index